Royal Murder

The Deadly Intrigue
of Ten Sovereigns

Elizabeth MacLeod

annick press
toronto + new york + vancouver

CONTENTS

Murder Most Royal

What's that in the shadow of the castle? That noise outside the king's office—is it a bomb? Is that the smell of gunpowder in the princess's dressing room? Who's lurking behind that throne?

Throughout the centuries, emperors, queens, tsars, and duchesses have lived with great wealth, responsibility—and danger. Murderers skulk everywhere, waiting for a chance to eliminate their royal targets. No matter how well monarchs are protected, they are never safe from a determined assassin. With so much power at stake, no wonder there are many fascinating, strange, and frightening tales of royal murders.

The main reason someone murders a royal is to grab the throne and assume all the wealth and power that go with it. The monarch's killer might be a subject—either a commoner or a noble—or another ruler. Cleopatra, Queen of Egypt, killed her royal brothers and sisters. Richard III of England has been accused of killing his brothers, nephews, and many others. Wallachia's Prince Vlad the Impaler—better known today as Dracula—killed his country's nobles, whom he judged untrustworthy. He also executed peasants who, in his opinion, didn't work hard enough.

> "I WANTED TO KILL A ROYALTY. IT DID NOT MATTER WHICH ONE."
>
> –LUIGI LUCHENI,
> ASSASSIN OF EMPRESS ELISABETH, 1898

Power makes some monarchs extremely distrustful of others, even paranoid. For that reason, one royal crime can easily lead to another. Mary, Queen of Scots and her allies are believed to have planned and successfully carried out the murder of her husband. Mary went on to hatch plots against her cousin, England's Queen Elizabeth I. Happily for Elizabeth, none of Mary's attempts were successful but that didn't stop her from trying.

It's easy to see how jealousy, greed, and hatred can result in a royal murder, but love can be just as lethal. Prince Dipendra of Nepal went on a killing rampage when he wasn't allowed to marry his chosen bride. Mary, Queen of Scots may have disposed of her husband so she could marry her lover—who just happened to be the likely murderer. King Faisal of Saudi Arabia was killed by his nephew because the king refused to punish the young man's beloved brother.

The assassin of Empress Elisabeth of Hungary didn't care which monarch he stabbed, as long as he took the life of someone who'd inherited the wealth and privilege he'd never experienced. Rebels are also willing to kill to bring about change. Sometimes mass uprisings occur when a large group of rebels feels oppressed and resents that a monarch has been born into power. This type of killing was especially popular in the late 1700s, with the deaths by guillotine of Louis XVI of France; his queen, Marie Antoinette; and other French nobles.

Killing royals for political reasons has been especially common since the late 1800s. Without a leader, a country can be thrown into chaos. Assassination was also seen as a way of bringing an end to the monarchy. It worked in Russia in 1918, with the execution of the czar and his family. Murdering monarchs has changed the course of history and affected the fortunes of countries and continents.

Once an assassin chooses a target, he or she must then choose a weapon. For a quick, quiet royal murder, a killer could choose among suffocation, poison, or a quick jab with a dagger. All of these methods required close access to the victim and steely nerves. As technology became more sophisticated, so did a murderer's choice of weapons. Guns, bombs, and grenades were added to the arsenal. They were effective and didn't require such close proximity to the victim. And they could have earth-shattering results: Austrian Archduke Franz Ferdinand's assassination in 1914 plunged the world into the First World War.

At one point, beheading was an effective and public way to murder a monarch. But royals also favored public forms of execution to send a harsh message to their people. Vlad the Impaler was horrifyingly inventive in the ways he found to murder people who displeased him. For hundreds of years, events such as beheadings and hangings were considered entertainment.

Some royal murderers have sought personal celebrity or have killed to raise awareness for a cause. Most of the assassination attempts against Queen Victoria were made by fame-seekers carrying guns that weren't even loaded. In more recent times, murdering a royal has sometimes been used to draw attention to a country's political situation. The illegal Irish Republican Army blew up Louis Mountbatten in 1979, not because he was powerful, but because he represented England, the country the terrorists felt was occupying their home.

If there is a mystery involved with a royal murder, there are often surprising developments. A person claiming to be the dead sovereign may appear years later, only to send experts scrambling to prove or disprove his or her identity. Impersonators of almost every member of the murdered Russian royal family came forward after the Russian Revolution. These amazing reappearances are often accompanied by tales of a sympathetic executioner who helped the "royal" escape, a loss of memory, or some other bizarre twist. In past centuries pretenders fooled many people, but now DNA matching can quickly determine whether a person is who he or she claims to be.

"I cannot be indifferent to the assassination of a member of my profession. We should be obliged to shut up business if we, the kings, were to consider the assassination of kings as of no consequence at all."

—ENGLAND'S KING EDWARD VII, 1903, AFTER THE MURDER OF KING ALEKSANDAR OF SERBIA

"When I despair, I remember that all through history the ways of truth and love have always won. There have been tyrants, and murderers, and for a time they can seem invincible, but in the end they always fall. Think of it—always."

—MAHATMA GANDHI

Some royal murders remain unsolved. For instance, did Boris III, czar of Bulgaria, die of natural causes—or did his refusal to cooperate with Adolf Hitler provoke the infamous Nazi leader to have Boris killed? And if Richard III of England didn't kill the two young princes who stood between him and the throne, who did? Despite advances in crime detection technology, it's still difficult to distinguish fact from fiction in many royal murders.

Get ready to read about some of history's deadliest assassins and most murderous royals. Their stories are shrouded in mystery or are full of incredible coincidences, while a number are shockingly grisly. You'll find out about murders that occurred more than 2,000 years ago, as well as others that are uncomfortably recent.

Some of these royals happened to be in the wrong place at the wrong time. Other monarchs killed so many of their subjects that a violent or early death should have come as no surprise to them. Whatever the case, in the stories that follow, you'll encounter both men and women who have been driven to commit the most violent act of all: murder.

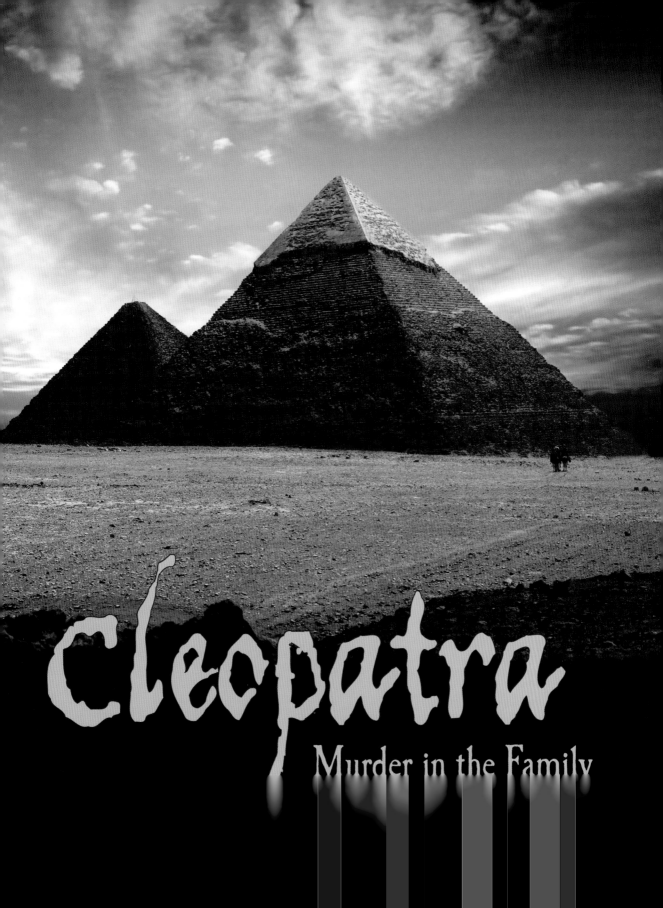

Cleopatra

Murder in the Family

Traitors!

thought a furious Princess Cleopatra. Her father had hardly left for Rome when her sisters Princess Berenice and Princess Cleopatra Tryphaena seized the chance to declare themselves queens of Egypt.

Cleopatra was only about 12 years old, but already she knew to keep her angry thoughts about her sisters to herself. Because she was clever as well as determined and ambitious, the queens wouldn't hesitate to eliminate her permanently if they sensed that she was less than totally loyal to them.

The thought made Cleopatra shiver. Her family, the Ptolemies, had a long history of fathers killing sons, wives assassinating husbands, and children eliminating parents and siblings. This murderous and bloody clan destroyed anyone who stood in the way of the throne. Egyptians called these killings the Curse of the Ptolemies. Because of it, Cleopatra grew up afraid—afraid of being poisoned or stabbed. The young girl already had her own food taster. Stories spread that the older Cleopatra—now queen—had tried to poison the younger one.

Born in about 69 BCE, Cleopatra was the third daughter of King Ptolemy XII. As well as two older sisters, she had a sister named Arsinoë, who was about two years younger than Cleopatra, and two younger brothers. Ptolemy XIII was about eight years younger than Cleopatra and Ptolemy XIV was about 10 years younger than she was. It was believed by their subjects and the family that they were descended from gods.

Cleopatra must have been very frightened about her future when, just a year into her father's absence and the reign of her two sisters, Cleopatra Tryphaena suddenly died. Queen Berenice seemed to be upset at the loss of her sibling, but rumors swirled that she had poisoned her sister with deadly mushrooms. Young Cleopatra decided it was vital to keep out of the queen's way and be as submissive and inconspicuous as possible. She must appear too childish and unimportant to kill. If only her father would return to Egypt and his throne!

When the queen's counselors insisted that she marry and share the throne with a man, she refused to marry her brother Ptolemy XIII. Berenice insisted on choosing her own husband and married a prince from Syria. However, he quickly displeased the hotheaded queen and was found strangled just three days after the wedding.

Soon Berenice had more problems. The reason her father, Ptolemy XII, had fled to Rome was because the Egyptian people were rioting against him. He'd promised huge bribes to Rome to buy the support and protection of the mighty Roman Empire. To raise the money for the bribes, Ptolemy taxed his subjects heavily. The people of Egypt didn't like Ptolemy's pro-Roman feelings, or the high taxes.

Ptolemy offered more money to the Romans if they would help put him back on the throne. They agreed—after all, it was the only way to get back their first payment. This time Ptolemy had to promise much more money, but he didn't mind. He figured he'd just tax his citizens further. Besides, the bigger the bribe Ptolemy owed the Romans, the harder they'd work to keep him on his throne.

In 55 BCE, Ptolemy, backed by Roman soldiers, returned to Egypt and dethroned Berenice. He quickly had her executed. With her two older sisters dead, Cleopatra was suddenly the next in line

Experts believe this may be Cleopatra but they're not sure. After she died, all statues of her were torn down. Some historians think she was plain looking, but her brains and charm made her irresistible.

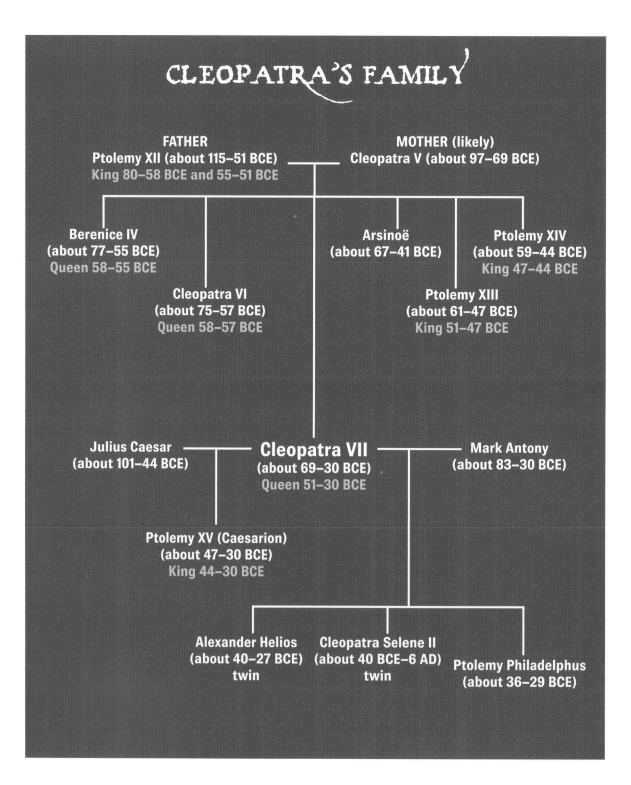

CLEOPATRA'S FAMILY

FATHER
Ptolemy XII (about 115–51 BCE)
King 80–58 BCE and 55–51 BCE

MOTHER (likely)
Cleopatra V (about 97–69 BCE)

Berenice IV
(about 77–55 BCE)
Queen 58–55 BCE

Cleopatra VI
(about 75–57 BCE)
Queen 58–57 BCE

Arsinoë
(about 67–41 BCE)

Ptolemy XIV
(about 59–44 BCE)
King 47–44 BCE

Ptolemy XIII
(about 61–47 BCE)
King 51–47 BCE

Julius Caesar
(about 101–44 BCE)

Cleopatra VII
(about 69–30 BCE)
Queen 51–30 BCE

Mark Antony
(about 83–30 BCE)

Ptolemy XV (Caesarion)
(about 47–30 BCE)
King 44–30 BCE

Alexander Helios
(about 40–27 BCE)
twin

Cleopatra Selene II
(about 40 BCE–6 AD)
twin

Ptolemy Philadelphus
(about 36–29 BCE)

to rule Egypt. She had gone from being an unimportant young princess to being heir to the throne—and she knew the dangers that could bring.

When her father became ill and died in 51 BCE, the country was in chaos. Cleopatra took over a nation that required a smart, determined ruler. She felt she was up to the job. There was just one problem. Ptolemy's will said that she must rule with her younger brother, Ptolemy XIII. The 18-year-old queen didn't want to share the throne with her 10-year-old brother. Besides, Berenice hadn't married her brother, so why should she?

Cleopatra acted as if she alone were the ruler of Egypt. Only her face appeared on the country's coins; her brother's wasn't included. Ptolemy's name was left off official documents. She excluded him from public ceremonies and made government decisions without consulting him.

Ptolemy XIII and his advisers were infuriated. They resented Cleopatra's independence and plotted to remove her from the throne so Ptolemy could rule alone. Every chance they got, they discredited her—even blaming a crop failure on her. Cleopatra felt lonely and threatened. Ptolemy's allies also claimed she was trying to give away the country to Rome, just as her father had done.

Actually, Cleopatra loved Egypt and was determined to keep it independent of Rome. Having grown up speaking Greek, she was one of the few Ptolemy rulers who bothered to learn to speak Egyptian so she could talk to her subjects. She admired her country's beauty and thought the city of Alexandria, where she lived, was the loveliest in the world. However, Cleopatra knew how strong Rome was and felt the only way Egypt could be successful and stable was to have Rome as an ally.

Cleopatra had only been queen for three years when, in 48 BCE, young Ptolemy's advisers forced her to flee for her life. She escaped to nearby Syria—but made sure she took plenty of jewels and money to finance an army. Cleopatra may have been forced out of Egypt for now, but she was determined to get back.

WHAT'S IN A NAME

It's hard to follow parts of Cleopatra's story because many of the people involved have the same name. For instance, all of the men in her family— including Cleopatra's father and her two brothers— were called Ptolemy, which is Greek for mighty in war.

The women in the Ptolemy family had a little more variety than the men when it came to names, but not much. They were all named Arsinoë (which means woman with uplifted mind), Berenice (bringer of victory), or Cleopatra (glory of her father).

Julius Caesar was an incredibly successful military commander thanks to his brilliant fighting strategies and his good relationship with his soldiers. He was also a great political leader and an excellent public speaker. Caesar was one of the most important men in world history and his name is reflected in the royal titles Kaiser, in Germany, and Czar in Russia.

Cleopatra's forces massed near the coast of the Mediterranean Sea, just beyond the border of Egypt, while her brother's army gathered nearby. Battle seemed inevitable. Each waited to see who would make the first move. Then fate intervened.

Elsewhere in the Mediterranean region, two Roman generals, Gaius Julius Caesar and Gnaeus Pompeius Magnus (known as Pompey), were fighting for control of Rome and its empire. When Pompey realized he was losing the war, he sailed to Egypt to ask for Ptolemy's help and protection. Caesar and his army followed in hot pursuit.

Ptolemy and his counselors had to make a tough choice. Should they help Pompey or support Caesar? Caesar looked more likely to win, so they decided to back him. But what to do with Pompey, who was asking for assistance? Ptolemy's side agreed to meet with Pompey but demanded that he arrive for the meeting alone. The general agreed. As soon as Pompey was in their clutches, they stabbed him to death.

Ptolemy decided to please Caesar, who by now had also arrived in Egypt, by sending him his enemy's head. But when Caesar received the horrible offering, he was appalled. Pompey had been a good soldier and a one-time friend. Furious, Caesar and his men marched into the royal city of Alexandria and took over the royal palace. He then demanded that Ptolemy and Cleopatra appear before him.

Ptolemy rushed to Alexandria. Having made one mistake, he didn't want to make another by keeping Caesar waiting. He also needed time to position his soldiers throughout the city before Cleopatra could arrive. Ptolemy's men were told to kill the exiled queen on sight. Then there'd be no question of sharing the throne with his sister.

Cleopatra's spies informed her of Ptolemy's schemes. She knew her throne and her life depended on her devising a foolproof plan to get to Caesar.

A few nights later, a fishing boat with a single rower appeared in the harbor of Alexandria. The rower tied up his boat, then hoisted the rolled-up rug lying in the bottom of the boat onto his shoulder. He trudged to the palace, where he was stopped by a sentry. The rug-bearer claimed he had a gift for Caesar and had to deliver it himself. He must have looked innocent because the soldier led him right to Caesar's room.

By this time, it was late at night. Caesar was amazed when the rug was unrolled and out sprang Cleopatra!

Caesar was impressed by the bold young queen. For her part, Cleopatra sensed the power of the man who is still known as one of the greatest generals in the world. She was only 18 and Caesar was almost 50. But the attraction between the two leaders was strong, and they immediately became lovers.

The next day Ptolemy met with Caesar—and Cleopatra. Ptolemy raged when he saw his sister and the way she had captivated Caesar. How had she managed to creep past his killers? Would this sister never stop plaguing him?

For Cleopatra, the meeting brought good news and bad news. Caesar announced that he was in Egypt to enforce the will of Cleopatra and Ptolemy's father, which meant that Ptolemy must share the throne with his sister. But Cleopatra's father had also said that she must marry her brother. That's what Ptolemies did, even if they didn't live together as a married couple— marriage was in name only. Cleopatra would have preferred to rule alone, but she was satisfied—for now. After all, the day before, Cleopatra had had only a desperate plan and a small army. Overnight, she'd become queen of Egypt again and had the most powerful man in the world as her ally.

But of course the brother and sister couldn't get along for long. Near the end of 48 BCE, one of Ptolemy's advisers secretly ordered his king's army to surround the royal palace, trapping Cleopatra, Caesar, and only a small army of Roman soldiers. Earlier, Caesar had arrested Ptolemy and made him live in the palace in order to keep his eye on the young king, so Ptolemy was imprisoned there too.

Meanwhile, another Ptolemy sibling was waiting to betray Cleopatra. Her younger sister, Arsinoë, decided to take advantage

NOT SO IMMORTAL

When Cleopatra's brother Ptolemy XIII drowned, Cleopatra commanded her soldiers to search the water for his body and not to stop until they'd found it. Since she hated him intensely, why was she so anxious to recover his body? There was a belief at the time that if someone drowned in the Nile and was never recovered, that person became immortal—a notion Cleopatra had to extinguish.

of Cleopatra's imprisonment to declare herself queen of Egypt. She slipped out of the palace and joined Ptolemy's army. Some Egyptians were unimpressed with both Ptolemy and Cleopatra but liked Arsinoë's wild ambition, and so they declared her the true queen. Soon she had killed the leader of Ptolemy's supporters and replaced him with a general she preferred.

Some of Caesar's army was trapped with him in the palace, but soon more of his soldiers arrived in Alexandria and began battling Ptolemy and Arsinoë's supporters. Cleopatra watched sadly from the palace as buildings were destroyed and ships burned in her beloved city. In the midst of it, Caesar actually allowed Ptolemy to leave the palace—perhaps Caesar hoped Ptolemy and Arsinoë would fight each other to the death, as most Ptolemy siblings did.

It was a close battle, but eventually Caesar's soldiers won. Ptolemy drowned during the attack, and Arsinoë was captured. Cleopatra was back on the throne of Egypt, this time with her even younger brother, Ptolemy XIV.

Although Caesar had a wife back in Rome and Cleopatra had just been married to her brother, the general and the queen lived in Egypt as a married couple. Cleopatra had a baby in about 47 BCE and named him Ptolemy XV or Caesarion, which means little Caesar. No child ever had a brighter future: his mother was the queen of Egypt and his father was a wildly successful general. No doubt Cleopatra dreamed of being ruler over Egypt and Rome alongside Caesar, with Caesarion taking over from both of them.

The next year Caesar had to return to Rome. Cleopatra and their son followed. Caesar wanted to impress Cleopatra with his success in battle, so he arranged for her to attend his triumphs—Roman events that honored a successful general or leader and showed the power of the Roman army. Treasure taken during the battle, as well as high-ranking

A triumph was a ceremony to honor a Roman military leader. It could include exotic animals and musicians, as well as slaves carrying looted treasure and signs showing images or names of conquered cities and people.

captives, were paraded before the people of Rome so they could glorify their army's might.

Cleopatra avoided most of the triumphs that celebrated Caesar's success in her beloved Egypt. But she did attend the one featuring his win over Ptolemy and Arsinoë. Cleopatra watched as Egyptian prisoners, including her captured sister, stumbled into the arena, struggling under the weight of their heavy chains. Cleopatra could see shame, anger, and desperation on Arsinoë's face. Both sisters knew that the parade would end very soon for Arsinoë, in a small dark room where she'd be strangled.

But Caesar was feeling generous, and at the last minute he pardoned Arsinoë, letting her live. She was exiled to a temple in faraway Ephesus (in modern-day Turkey). Cleopatra suspected that her sister would not have been so merciful. And in her heart, Cleopatra knew the only way her sister would no longer be a danger to her was if she was dead.

While in Rome, Cleopatra lived just outside the city, and Caesar visited her often. He showered her with gifts and even built a statue of her in a temple. The people of Rome disliked Cleopatra because she wasn't Roman and because she had seduced their top general. They were scandalized by her extravagant ways and many servants.

When rumors started that Caesar not only intended to pass a law allowing him to marry Cleopatra, but that he also planned to make

MIDDLE OF MARCH

Shortly before Caesar was stabbed to death, he visited a soothsayer to have his future predicted. "Beware the Ides of March," warned the fortune-teller. Since then, the term *Ides of March* has meant a day of doom. But ides didn't have any special meaning during Caesar's time. It was just a way of referring to the middle of the month.

Too bad for Caesar that he didn't heed the prediction. On March 15, as he was heading to a meeting, he saw the soothsayer again and laughingly said, "The Ides of March are come." "Yes, they are come," replied the soothsayer, "but they are not past ..."

himself king of Rome, some powerful politicians decided that he must be stopped.

At a meeting on March 15, 44 BCE, Caesar was brutally stabbed and killed by a group of assassins. Cleopatra knew she was hated in Rome. With her protector assassinated, she realized that she and Caesarion were in grave danger, but before they could be seized by Caesar's enemies, Cleopatra and her son escaped back to Egypt.

There, rumors started to fly when Cleopatra's remaining brother died suddenly. His mysterious death was blamed on poisoning by Cleopatra. After all, Ptolemy was 15, and in Cleopatra's world that was old enough for her to fear a challenge from him for control of Egypt. As well, he was the only person who stood between Cleopatra's son and the country's throne. Soon after Ptolemy's death, Cleopatra declared her son co-ruler with her. This was the first step in her campaign to make Caesarion ruler over both Egypt and Rome. (Governing Rome might have seemed impossible at that point, but after all, the ambitious Cleopatra probably reasoned, he *was* Caesar's son.)

Cleopatra had other family troubles: her sister Arsinoë. Although she was in exile, her supporters were once more scheming to put her on Egypt's throne.

Now that Rome had lost its great general, battle broke out across the empire to decide who would succeed him. Eventually the vast Roman Empire was divided among three leaders: Gaius Octavianus (known as Octavian; he was Caesar's great-nephew), Marcus Aemilius Lepidus, and Marcus Antonius (or Mark Antony). Antony took the eastern part of the empire, which included Egypt. To maintain and extend the empire, he knew he needed Egypt's help. So, in 41 BCE, he sent a messenger demanding that Cleopatra meet with him immediately in Tarsus (in today's Turkey).

How did a general dare to command a queen? Antony knew that Rome was continuing to expand and become more powerful.

He was also aware that Egypt's strength was failing, thanks to the lavish spending of Cleopatra's father, and the fighting among her siblings. As well, almost 100 years before Cleopatra was born, one of her ancestors had made Rome a "guardian" of Egypt. That was why in Cleopatra's time Caesar, as Rome's representative, had had the power to decide that she and her brother would rule in Egypt. No wonder Antony believed that all he had to do was tell Cleopatra where and when to meet him and she would meekly show up.

But Cleopatra felt very differently. She wasn't used to being ordered around. After all, not only was she a queen but she was also descended from gods. She may have needed Rome's help but she knew that Rome needed Egypt for its money and grain. So Cleopatra decided to meet with Antony but at a time that she chose, not when he told her to appear. Antony had also included in his message the suggestion that she should come in "all the splendor her art could command." He didn't know what he was in for.

When Antony finally got word that the queen had arrived in Tarsus, he smugly waited in the city's marketplace. He believed that Cleopatra and her court would come and present themselves to him. But Antony gradually realized that the marketplace and the streets surrounding it were empty. Everyone in the town had flocked to the harbor to see Cleopatra's amazing arrival.

An ancient historian recorded that Cleopatra sailed into Tarsus in a golden ship, "its purple sails billowing in the wind, while her rowers caressed the water with oars of silver which dipped in time to the music of the flute, accompanied by pipes and lutes. Cleopatra herself reclined beneath a canopy of cloth of gold, dressed in the character of Venus." When Antony arrived at the harbor, he was overwhelmed by the magnificence of Cleopatra's ship, as well as by the sumptuous meals she served him aboard the boat. It's hardly surprising that the pair soon became lovers.

WEAPON OF CHOICE

Simple to use and easy to conceal—no wonder Cleopatra, Mark Antony, and Caesar's assassins all carried daggers. They were some of the earliest weapons prehistoric people created, although, unlike Antony's metal dagger, early ones were made of flint, ivory, and even bone.

Daggers are used for stabbing or cutting. These double-edged knives were associated with cowardliness and deceit because they could be hidden or used from behind. But they could also indicate bravery, since assassins had to get quite close to their victims to kill them with a dagger. Until recently, military leaders throughout history wore decorative daggers as symbols of power.

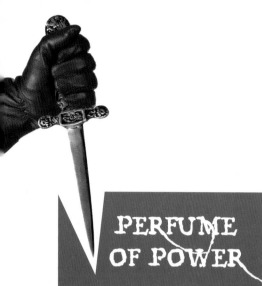

PERFUME OF POWER

As Cleopatra sailed into Tarsus, she ordered her servants to perfume the sails of her boat. As well, sweet-smelling smoke drifted from the ship's incense burners. The people watching onshore not only saw an incredible spectacle and heard beautiful music from the boat's musicians, but also were overwhelmed by the fantastic odors. Cleopatra wanted to appeal to as many of the observers' senses as possible. As well, she wished to remind everyone that Egypt was known around the world for its rich and exotic perfumes.

Recently, a chemist reconstructed the perfume Cleopatra supposedly wore the first time she met Mark Antony. It was made of many costly ingredients, including saffron, the world's most expensive spice. Today Cleopatra's scent would be one of the most expensive perfumes available.

Cleopatra had set out to win over Antony for a number of reasons. First, she'd come to Tarsus to do business with him. Egypt was rich thanks to the grain and other goods it sold to various nations. Cleopatra dipped into the country's treasury to spend lavishly on delectable food and extravagant luxuries to impress Antony because in her mind they were an investment in this business relationship.

Secondly, Cleopatra thought that a personal relationship with Antony would maintain Egypt's independence from Rome. More importantly, it would keep her on the throne. She was right: Antony agreed that Egypt would remain an independent country, rather than become part of the Roman empire, and that Cleopatra would continue to rule the country. In return, she would supply Antony with the money and goods he needed. As well, Antony would protect Cleopatra from her enemies. That included her sister Arsinoë. It wasn't long before the exiled princess was executed by Antony's men.

Now there was only one survivor of all of Ptolemy XII's six children: Cleopatra. She'd had a hand in three of the deaths: one brother had died in combat with her allies, the other was probably poisoned by her, and she'd arranged for Arsinoë's assassination. The Curse of the Ptolemies had decimated another generation. And there were more deaths to come for the sole remaining member of Egypt's royal family.

Cleopatra returned to Alexandria, and Antony soon followed. He spent a year with her. Shortly after he returned to Rome, their twin children, Alexander Helios and Cleopatra Selene II, were born.

For three years, Cleopatra didn't see Antony. In 37 BCE, on his way to battle in Parthia (part of today's Iran), Antony stopped in Alexandria for a brief visit. He was captivated once again. Cleopatra's charms were enough to make him race through the war and hurry back to Egypt. Antony and

Cleopatra were married in 36 BCE, despite the fact that he was already married, to Octavian's sister, Octavia. Ptolemy Philadephus, another son for Antony and Cleopatra, was born later that year.

Octavian was angry about the way Octavia had been treated. But he had another reason to target Mark Antony—Octavian had recently forced Lepidus, the empire's third ruler, into exile. If he could just get rid of Mark Antony, then the whole Roman Empire would be his. So in 32 BCE, Octavian declared war on Cleopatra, knowing that he was also declaring war on Antony.

The next year, the two sides met off the coast of Greece. Antony and Cleopatra's army and navy far out-numbered Octavian's, but Octavian's men were led by a skilled admiral. As well, although Antony was much more experienced at fighting on land, Cleopatra insisted on a sea battle, so that she could remain with both her ships and with Antony.

The boats on the opposing sides were locked in battle when Cleopatra and a group of her ships slipped through the opposing forces and raced for Egypt. Although this was part of Antony and Cleopatra's plan—Cleopatra's ships were full of Egyptian gold and jewels—Antony's troops were astounded when he left the battle and followed her. Antony and Cleopatra's soldiers fought hard, but Octavian won the battle.

Cleopatra knew Octavian would invade Egypt, so she prepared by putting on a great show of strength and boldness. The lavish ceremonies she held maintained her image as a powerful queen. In case that didn't work, she also sent gifts of great value to Octavian, asking him to let her live and allow her sons to reign in Egypt. Octavian accepted the gifts but promised to pardon her only if she killed Antony. Cleopatra refused.

VISIT CLEOPATRA

The Ptolemy palace where Cleopatra lived in Alexandria was one of the most spectacular and luxurious buildings ever created. Its beautiful large rooms were decorated with gold and marble, and the gardens that surrounded it were gorgeous and lush with tall trees and beautiful pathways.

If you want to visit Cleopatra's palace today, you'll first have to slip on a diving suit and scuba tanks. The island where the palace stood, as well as most of ancient Alexandria, collapsed into the sea hundreds of years ago after a series of earthquakes and tidal waves.

In the 1990s, a French team began exploring the sea floor off Alexandria. To see through the filthy, polluted water of the harbor, they used Global Positioning System (GPS) technology, sonar devices, and other high-tech equipment. The underwater archeologists believe they have located Cleopatra's palace and someday hope to set up an underwater museum at the site. Visitors may one day walk through glass tunnels to get up close to Cleopatra's life and home.

The queen then hid gold, jewels, and other treasures in a royal tomb. If a world empire ruled by Rome and Egypt was now out of Cleopatra's grasp, she'd make sure she had the resources to keep Egypt if she could. Perhaps she would use her treasure to found a new kingdom elsewhere, beyond the reach of the Romans. With that in mind, she sent her son Caesarion in the direction of India with a portion of the royal treasury.

At the end of July 30 BCE, Octavian and his army arrived in Egypt to finish off Antony and Cleopatra. When dawn broke on August 1, Antony took his place at the head of what was left of his troops. Cleopatra may have been watching from the windows of her palace, just the way she had watched years before when Caesar's forces fought in the streets of Alexandria. As Antony and Cleopatra's ships advanced out of Alexandria's harbor to meet Octavian's fleet, Antony was shocked to see the vessels desert to Octavian's side. The cavalry also joined the enemy, while the infantry scattered.

Desperate, Antony fled to Cleopatra's palace, but when he arrived, the queen was nowhere to be found. Then Antony received the message that she was dead! With his power, army, and now his great love gone, he had no reason to live. He pulled out his sword and stabbed himself.

As Antony lay bleeding to death, he received word that Cleopatra wasn't dead: she had barricaded herself in her tomb. Too weak to walk, Antony ordered slaves to carry him to her. Cleopatra was desperate to embrace Antony one last time but feared that Octavian's men would force their way in if she opened the door of the tomb to admit him. So she and her servants hoisted the dying Antony on ropes up to a window of her temple. Cleopatra was soon covered with his blood as he died in her arms.

Almost immediately, Octavian's men were hammering on the grief-stricken queen's door. She refused to let them enter. However, one soldier distracted her while others stealthily

Cleopatra was heartbroken to learn that Antony had stabbed himself. However she kept her head and figured out a way to allow Antony to join her in her tomb, yet not let in Octavian's men. It must have been incredibly painful for Antony to be hauled up to Cleopatra (far right), but he had to see her one last time.

"I WILL NOT BE TRIUMPHED OVER."

—CLEOPATRA, 30 BCE

climbed ladders to sneak in a window. As they tried to grab Cleopatra, she quickly pulled out a dagger to stab herself. But the soldiers overpowered her, and she became Octavian's prisoner.

Cleopatra knew what lay ahead. She thought back to that afternoon in the Roman arena long ago when she sat by Caesar's side watching Arsinoë shuffle by. She remembered her sister's shame as she paraded past the jeering Romans. Never, thought the proud queen. I'd rather die than let Octavian parade me in a triumph. Thanks to Octavian, she had lost her throne, her country, and her lover. But Cleopatra herself was determined to remain unconquered.

Octavian and Cleopatra were locked in battle again: he wanted to keep her alive so the people of Rome could mock her, and she was determined to die. Cleopatra tried to starve herself, but Octavian sent word that unless she ate, he would kill Antony's and her three children, so Cleopatra began eating again.

What could Cleopatra do now? She and Octavian were scheduled to leave for Rome on August 15. Three days before that, Cleopatra began putting a plan into action. She asked Octavian to allow her one last visit to Antony's tomb before she left her country forever. Octavian believed she'd accepted the fate he had in store for her and granted her request.

Following her tearful visit to Antony's tomb, Cleopatra returned to her own monument, where she bathed and dressed in her most sumptuous royal gowns. Then she ordered an elaborate feast, including fresh figs that were brought to her in a basket. When Cleopatra had finished eating, she dispatched a letter to Octavian, then dismissed all but her two most trusted servant women.

When Octavian received Cleopatra's letter, he read her request that she be buried with Antony. Had she tricked him and found a way to kill herself? Octavian sent his officers racing to her tomb to stop her, but they were too late. There, stretched out on a bed of gold, was Cleopatra, stone dead, her servants dying at her feet.

Coiled under the figs that had been brought to the queen was an asp, or Egyptian cobra. Cleopatra knew that the bite of this

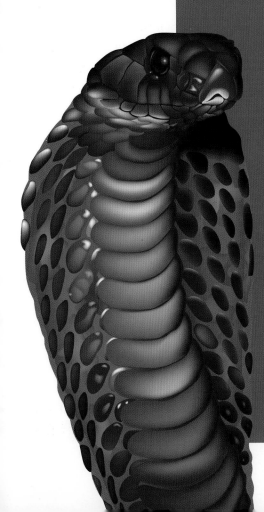

DEADLY SERPENT

As soon as Cleopatra realized she couldn't escape from Octavian, she began planning her death. She already knew the bite of an asp, or Egyptian cobra, is deadly—legend says that she tested deadly poisons on animals or condemned prisoners for her entertainment. After all, growing up in such a dangerous family, Cleopatra knew she needed to be prepared.

The asp is the snake often pictured rising up out of a snake charmer's basket. It's one of the most poisonous snakes and kills many people every year. When the asp is angry or disturbed, it flares out the loose skin of its neck into a hood. The asp won't bite unless it's threatened but then will attack again and again until it can escape.

The asp's venom is neurotoxic, which means it destroys nerve tissue. Victims quickly become paralyzed and unable to breathe. Cleopatra would have known that the venom of a viper would have left her swollen and unattractive, but an asp's bite gave her little pain or stress. She simply fell into a coma and died calmly and beautifully.

Cleopatra didn't choose death by asp bite just because of its speed and ease. A stylized version of the asp was the symbol of royal power in Egypt. She knew people would tell and retell the story of her death. By allowing this emblem of divine sovereignty to bite her, Cleopatra—and her subjects— believed she would become immortal.

snake brought quick, painless death, so she had secretly arranged for the serpent to be hidden in the basket of figs. She had cheated Octavian out of his victorious return to Rome with his royal prisoner.

The last pharaoh of Egypt was gone. The deadly Curse of the Ptolemies took its final victim. Despite Cleopatra's ruthlessness, she had loved her country and kept it mostly at peace while she was on the throne. At a time when most women had little power, Cleopatra ambitiously challenged great male leaders for control. More than 2,000 years after her death, people are still fascinated by this cunning, determined, and irresistible woman.

Cleopatra's two maids died with her. When Octavian's men rushed in, Iras was already sprawled dead on the floor and Charmion remained standing for only a few more moments.

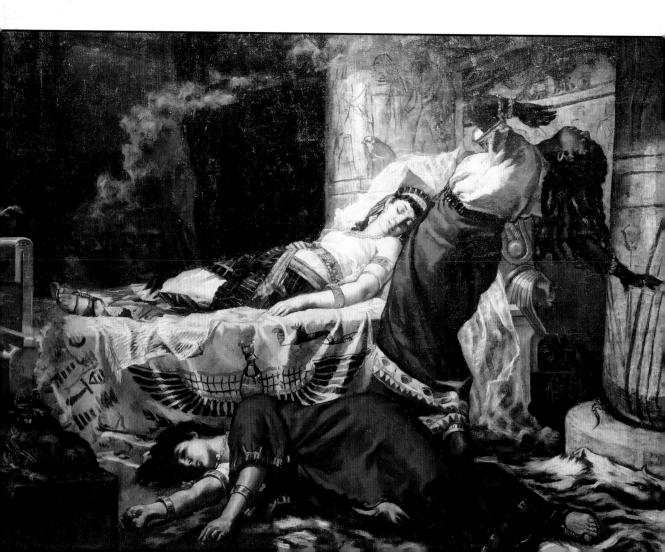

Vlad Ţepeş

Blood-Crazed Avenger

Thud!

The 11-year-old Vlad landed with a crash on the cold stone floor. Before he could scramble to his feet, the heavy door of his prison cell clanged shut. Vlad was now the prisoner of Sultan Murad of Turkey, to make sure the boy's father remained loyal to the Turkish leader. The 1400s were a time of constant war and invasions, and hostage-taking was a way of life among armies and their leaders.

Vlad's father, also named Vlad, ruled Wallachia, now part of Romania, in Eastern Europe. This prince was a ruthless fighter and a member of the Order of the Dragon, a powerful group of knights. The dragon was a symbol of destruction and force that struck terror into the hearts of the fighters' enemies. Because of this military honor, Vlad was called Dracul, Romanian for "the dragon"—and "the devil." Young Vlad shared his father's nickname, but the letter *a* was added, which in Romanian means "son of." The young boy Dracula had a name that more than 500 years later still sends shivers down people's spines.

Even as a child, Vlad showed signs of the heartless murderer he would later become. The house where he was born in Wallachia looked out on the square where criminals were hanged. Vlad watched executions for hours from his bedroom window.

Wallachia suffered from constant threats, either from the Turks to the south or from the Hungarians to the west. Vlad's father sided with whichever side he thought would help him stay on his throne. No wonder Sultan Murad didn't trust him as an ally. When Vlad Dracul met with the sultan in 1442, the Wallachian prince must have suspected he and his sons (Vlad and seven-year-old Radu) were about to be imprisoned. So he left behind in Wallachia his oldest son, Mircea. It was clear to young Vlad that Mircea was his father's favorite—after all, Mircea's life wasn't risked as a hostage. Vlad was consumed by resentment toward his father and older brother.

Vlad Dracul was forced to stay in Turkey for a year, but his two sons were held there for six years. Although the boys were

VISIT VLAD

Castle Dracula, where Vlad once lived, is now in ruins. However, you can still visit Bran Castle, a fortress where he sometimes stayed. The fortress is named for the town where it's located and is one of Romania's top tourist destinations. Often referred to as Dracula's Castle, it houses a museum of furniture and art dating back as far as the 1300s.

In această casă a locuit
intre anii 1431–1435,
domnitorul Țării Romănești

VLAD DRACUL,

fiul lui
Mircea cel Bătrin.

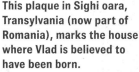

This plaque in Sighi oara, Transylvania (now part of Romania), marks the house where Vlad is believed to have been born.

sometimes imprisoned in an underground dungeon, at other times they were treated well. It all depended on how they behaved and how loyal his father and Mircea were to the sultan. Radu was a good-looking boy and obedient, while Vlad was skinny, socially awkward, and often threw temper tantrums.

Vlad felt abandoned by his whole family. The Turkish customs, religion, and language were also strange to him. Even when the sultan acted as if the boys were guests rather than prisoners, Vlad knew his life was in danger. Two other young princes whom the sultan had judged to be traitors had been blinded with red-hot pokers—even though their sister was married to the sultan! Vlad saw many other tortures and executions. At such a young age with no parents in a foreign country, the horrors he watched must have affected him.

Then Vlad received word that his father was encouraging Mircea to cooperate with the sultan's enemies. The teenager knew his future

was precarious, and the terms of his imprisonment became even harsher. He learned from his father's actions that human life was cheap and expendable. Luckily for Vlad, the sultan felt the boy had more value alive than dead, so he used him against Vlad's father.

When Vlad was sixteen, his father was decapitated by his noblemen, or boyars, because he supported Turkey. The boyars also blinded Vlad's older brother, Mircea. Who would now rule Wallachia? The Turkish leader forced his way into the country and put young Vlad on the throne. But before long the Hungarian army invaded Wallachia and threw out the Turks. After just two months of wearing the crown that Vlad felt was his to inherit, he had to flee for his life. The young ruler vowed that he'd be back.

Vlad headed to the nearby country of Moldavia, where his cousin was in power. But the cousin was assassinated, so for the next few years, Vlad was often on the run. In constant danger and always suspicious, the young man became more distrustful and vengeful.

Vlad decided to take his chances in Hungary, even though that country had recently been his enemy. It was a worthwhile gamble. The Hungarians pardoned Vlad for his previous disloyalty— perhaps because Vlad's family for generations had tended to side with Hungary—and agreed to support his bid for the Wallachian throne.

With an army of supporters, Vlad invaded Wallachia in 1456. He met the current prince in hand-to-hand combat, hacked him to death—a typical end for a battle in those days—and took over the throne. Finally, he was Vlad III of Wallachia, ruler again in his native country.

Not surprisingly, Vlad didn't feel secure on the throne, so he set about eliminating any threats to his power. Since he no longer trusted the boyars who had killed his father and brother, Vlad chose lesser-known people and a few foreigners as his new

LADY DRACULA

Erzsébet Báthory, a countess who lived in present-day Slovakia, was as bloodthirsty as Vlad. Around 1600, she tortured and killed young women—the more noble the better. Erzsébet was finally captured and imprisoned in 1611.

For three years, this murderous aristocrat lived in a cell, seeing no one—her food was pushed through a small hole in the thick stone wall that surrounded her. When her jailer one day found the food uneaten, he knew the Blood Countess was dead.

Erzsébet may have killed hundreds or thousands of victims and is known as the deadliest serial murderer in history.

Short, stocky, and strong—
Vlad was all of these things.
His neck was thick and his
shoulders were wide. Vlad's
long straight nose and large
nostrils make him look especially cruel and threatening.

advisers. Some of these people were inexperienced, but they all promised to be loyal to their
ruler. If not, Vlad got rid of them so he could
maintain absolute control over his country and
stand against invaders.

According to the stories Vlad's enemies told
about him, Vlad kept his hold on power primarily through torture and executions. One of his
favorite methods was impalement, which he'd
learned years earlier when he was imprisoned.

The victim had a stake forced up through
his body until it emerged from his mouth.
Usually death took hours or days, and the bodies
were often left on public display for months
until they were well decayed. The monarch
became so well known for this horrible practice
that people began calling him Vlad Țepeș (pro-
nounced TSE-pesh), which means Vlad the
Impaler.

Thousands might be impaled at one time.
In 1460, for example, Vlad is said to have
punished the city of Sibiu, Transylvania. The

citizens had sometimes helped challengers to his throne. So Vlad had 10,000 townspeople impaled. Then he had their stakes arranged in circles around the city.

Impalement may have been the method of torture that Vlad preferred, but it wasn't his only one. Legends say he loved to watch as his henchmen burned his victims to death, cut off arms and legs, boiled wrongdoers alive, or skinned them. Nobles and peasants, women and children, foreigners, and long-time citizens all suffered at his hands. However, most of Vlad's victims were businessmen and noblemen from Transylvania and Wallachia. Some of these were the boyars who had killed his father and older brother.

Vlad also believed the nobles took advantage of hard-working farmers and others. Once Vlad invited many nobles to a grand dinner. In the middle of the feast, he arrested them all. The older ones and their families were impaled immediately. The younger, stronger nobles and their families were marched north to a castle that Vlad wanted rebuilt. The story goes that they worked so hard and for so long that their clothes fell off. After that, they were forced to work naked, no matter how bitter the weather. Very few of them survived the rebuilding of what became known as Castle Dracula.

Although Vlad made donations to many churches and monasteries, even the religious were not exempt from his cruelty. At one point he tried to convert a monastery into a prison and torture chamber. In a tiny cell, Vlad piously

Legends tell how Vlad liked to eat his meals in the midst of all of the gore and misery of his impaled victims. It is said that he sometimes forced others to join him at his table.

invited his victim to kneel and pray in front of an altar. While the prisoner was saying his prayers, a trap door suddenly opened beneath him. Kicking and screaming, the victim dropped into a hole below onto poles placed to pierce his body.

Vlad's term of terror lasted for six years. Except for his horrific acts of cruelty, he spent his time the way many rulers did. He traveled around his country, setting laws and heading important court trials, as well as meeting with diplomats from other countries and making public appearances on special occasions.

Building up his country, especially its agricultural systems, was vital to Vlad because he knew he needed a stable country to have any chance of fending off armies from Turkey and Hungary, which were always threatening Wallachia. Vlad's troops fought many times against the Turks, and at least 100,000 Turkish fighters were impaled.

In 1462, the Turkish army occupied Târgoviflte, in the middle of today's Romania, and Vlad was chased to Transylvania. As he and his army fled, they burned villages and crops to the ground so the enemies pursuing them would find no food or supplies. Of course, neither would the peasants who lived in the villages. The Impaler and his men pushed animal corpses into wells to contaminate them and dug pits lined with sharp stakes to catch any careless horse riders.

Once Vlad arrived in Transylvania, the Hungarians, his sometime allies, who were in power there, imprisoned him. While in jail, he was able to continue his cruel practices. He captured mice and birds and tortured them. It's hard to imagine, but somehow Vlad could also be charming when he chose to be. Not only did he convince the Hungarian monarch to release him from prison, but he was allowed to marry a cousin of the king. He and his new wife lived in Hungary until the mid-1470s.

Vlad continued to be cruel and unpredictable. One day a criminal ran into his courtyard to escape the mob that was

VLAD AND THE BRITISH THRONE

Britain's Queen Elizabeth II and her family are related to Vlad the Impaler. Elizabeth's grandmother Queen Mary was descended from many royal Hungarian and Romanian families, including Vlad's.

VLAD ON VIDEO

Not many people today would know about Vlad if it hadn't been for British writer Bram Stoker, who was inspired by the legends about the bloodthirsty ruler. Stoker's book *Dracula*, published in 1897, wasn't the first about vampires. But Stoker wove together a wicked nobleman, a beautiful but wild country, and the folk tradition about vampires to create a best seller.

For the first seven years of his life, Stoker languished in bed with a strange illness that was never diagnosed. Later, his mother told him terrifying stories about a cholera epidemic that had swept through her neighborhood when she was young. This very infectious stomach disease killed many, seemingly without warning.

Stoker drew on both of these events to make the vampire attacks in his book, and their symptoms, seem weird and mysterious. He set parts of the book in the English town of Whitby, where he was living. He was also inspired by the abbey there (below, left).

The first film version of the Dracula story was a black-and-white silent movie released in 1921 called *Nosferatu* (left). Stoker's widow refused to let anyone make a movie based on her husband's book, so the movie-maker couldn't use the book's title. *Nosferatu* means "the unclean one" or "the devil" in Romanian. This movie added supernatural abilities to Dracula's talents—the main character could dissolve into a mist and disappear.

Dracula, the English-language vampire movie filmed in 1931, is now considered a classic. The actor Béla Lugosi was a terrifying vampire, even though he didn't really understand the lines he was performing. That's because he hardly spoke English—he was born in what's now Romania, Dracula's country.

More than 160 movies feature Dracula as a main character. That makes him second in popularity as a subject only to the famous fictitious detective Sherlock Holmes!

chasing him. A policeman in hot pursuit had just grabbed the crook when Vlad suddenly cut off the officer's head with his sword. When asked to explain himself, the murderous prince replied, "I did not commit a crime. [The officer] committed suicide. Anyone will perish in this way should he thievingly invade the house of a great sovereign." It's hard to believe, but the Hungarian ruler was impressed by Vlad's courage and simply laughed at his reply.

Around 1475, Vlad the Impaler was ready to make another bid for the throne of Wallachia, this time with a mixed force of Wallachians, Transylvanians, and Moldavians. Vlad liked to attack at night. To the people of Wallachia it must have seemed as if he was coming back from the dead to reclaim his inheritance.

At this point, the Turkish leader Basarab was on the throne of Wallachia. He'd heard the stories of Vlad's cruelty, and when Basarab learned about the approaching army, he and his allies fled the country. Vlad was back on the throne again but had little support to remain there. Not surprisingly, his cruelty had turned his country's people against him. When the Turks attacked in 1476, Vlad's army was far outnumbered.

There are numerous stories about how he died. Some say he was killed in battle. One legend says that one of his own soldiers mistook him for the enemy and struck him with a lance. Another tale says that some noblemen assassinated him or that he was murdered by a Turk who was one of his servants. Most stories agree that Vlad's body was beheaded and sent to Istanbul. There, the

THE GOLDEN CUP

Vlad insisted on honesty and order. Any lawbreakers in his kingdom knew they would be murdered in some grisly way. As a result, very few thieves dared to steal anything within this royal's domain. Vlad was so certain of people's fear of him that he placed a golden cup in the main square of the capital city and said everyone could drink from it. The cup was never stolen—at least not while Vlad was on the throne.

Turkish leader displayed it high on a stake to show that Vlad's cruel reign was over.

Throughout his life, Vlad probably murdered hundreds of thousands of people. He lived during a bloody time in a violent area. Some Romanian peasants later remembered him as a ruler who defended his country, which was always under siege by the Turks and Hungarians. As well, Vlad championed peasants' rights by making sure that nobles didn't take advantage of their labor. Fear of Vlad's cruel tortures also kept the boyars from becoming overly wealthy and powerful.

Many people have suggested that Vlad must have been insane. He had extreme reactions to even the smallest wrong. He believed that horrific consequences were the only way to maintain law and order and to improve his homeland's economy.

There's no doubt that Vlad was a ruthless killer, but it's difficult to determine whether all the horrific stories about him can be true. Most of the legends were passed down by his enemies, who likely exaggerated his cruelty. As well, the printing press was just becoming popular in Europe during Vlad's reign and printers were looking for sensational stories to sell. Vlad gave them plenty to report. The gore and bloodiness of the sagas ensured the tales would be best sellers. The incredible stories told of his life still fascinate people more than 500 years later.

Back and forth, back and forth. As Richard paced his room, he feverishly pondered what he should do. He'd always loved his brother King Edward IV—now gravely ill—and wanted to see Edward's son inherit England's throne. But Richard also loved England and knew that an unprepared 12-year-old monarch was one of the worst possible leaders for a country in search of peace and stability. A child king such as Edward's young son was weak, and could be easily influenced, just when England needed a strong, well-trained monarch. Why did Edward have to die right now, worried Richard bitterly.

The year 1483 was a turbulent time in English history. For almost thirty years the Wars of the Roses had raged throughout the country. Battles were constantly being fought between two sides, the supporters of the House of York (Edward and Richard's family) and the House of Lancaster. The civil wars got their name because the York side wore white coats or a white rose symbol, while the Lancaster allies wore red coats or red roses.

At the end of 1460, when Richard was just eight, his brother Edmund and their father were killed in battle. A few months later, the young boy's 19-year-old brother Edward seized the throne from Lancastrian King Henry VI and became King Edward IV. Richard and his fourth brother, George, were made dukes. As was the custom in those times, Richard was sent away to learn how to joust and hunt. He became a brave, skilled soldier, although he had a reputation for recklessness.

In 1470, the Lancastrians overpowered Edward IV, and he was exiled to Europe. Being a loyal brother, Richard accompanied the banished king. Richard's admiration and support of his brother was unusual in such a murderous, power-hungry time. When Edward and Richard returned to England the next year, they defeated Henry VI's forces. Edward grabbed the crown once more.

Although Henry survived the battle that cost him his crown, he was sent to the Tower of London, where he was murdered a

The "Wars of the Roses" took place between 1455 and 1485 but the term probably wasn't used for the battles until the 1800s.

few days later. When Richard's enemies were trying to blacken his reputation, Henry's death was blamed on Richard. But it's more likely that Edward was behind Henry's death. In those days only a monarch could order the death of another monarch. The new king may have seen Henry's murder as a necessity to prevent Henry's allies from rallying around the former ruler. But later it would generate a lot of gossip. Even though Henry's son was killed in battle in 1471, a rumor started that Richard and his brother Edward had murdered him.

Edward assigned Richard to administer the north of England, though he was less than 20 years old. At the time, Scotland often battled England for territory, so Richard and his troops fought frequently to protect England's borders. Nevertheless, there was more peace in the country than there had been for many years.

But trouble was soon brewing again. For years, Henry and Richard's brother, George, had been trying to put himself on England's throne. By 1478, he had annoyed King Edward once too often with his plots and schemes. George was charged with being a traitor by the English parliament and sent to the Tower of London. Treason was a serious crime, and George was sentenced to death. Thanks to his noble birth, he was killed privately rather than in public. Some people later blamed Richard for George's death, saying that because Richard was younger, he'd killed his brother to put himself one step closer to the throne. The accusation was made even though Richard was far away in the north of England when it happened. George's execution was most certainly Edward's responsibility, but that didn't halt the rumors.

All calm in the country vanished in April 1483 when King Edward suddenly became very ill—likely from pneumonia, although some claimed he'd been poisoned. Before he died, the king just had time to name Richard the protector of his 12-year-old son, also named Edward. As protector, Richard would act as king until Edward V grew up, but Richard wouldn't actually

DEATH BY WINE

No one knows for sure how Richard's brother George died once he was taken to the Tower of London. One story says he was drowned in a large cask of strong wine. The alcohol fumes alone from so much wine would easily knock him unconscious.

Richard is painted here wearing elaborate robes and jewelry to show his great wealth. His hands draw attention to a ring that likely represents the coronation ring and stresses his position as king.

have the title of monarch. Then Richard learned that Edward's mother, Elizabeth, planned to have her son quickly crowned and to exclude Richard. She didn't want to lose any of her power as the king's mother to his uncle. She and her many relatives formed a formidable force against the boy's protector. Richard feared they would isolate the boy from him and take as much power as possible into their own hands. Many English lords and nobles were on Richard's side and agreed he should assume his position as protector.

Richard raced south from the Scottish border to meet his nephew and escort him to London, where he was to be crowned. Already accompanying Edward V en route was an uncle on his mother's side, Earl Rivers. Richard had Rivers and three others arrested, then Richard accompanied Edward V to the Tower of London—it was a palace in those days, as well as a prison— where Richard could ensure his nephew's safekeeping. As preparations for Edward's coronation proceeded, Richard persuaded Elizabeth to allow Edward's younger brother, Richard, to join them at the Tower of London so he could be company for the young king.

Suddenly a priest came forward with a startling revelation about young Edward's father. The holy man claimed that there had been an agreement between Edward IV and another woman before Edward married Elizabeth. In those days, this was like a marriage. If what the priest said was true, it meant that Edward IV's children by this "second" wife were illegitimate and therefore unable to inherit the throne. It also meant that Richard was next in line for England's crown.

Had Edward made an agreement with another woman before marrying Elizabeth, people wondered. Or had Richard somehow forced the priest to make this declaration? There were rumors of a document but never any definite evidence of it. However, perhaps Richard's claim to the throne was for more than just his personal gain. He knew that Henry VI had come to

LIKE FATHER, LIKE SON

Hundreds of years ago, when a ruler died, many claimed the throne and were willing to kill for it. The tradition of passing the crown from father to son was created to reduce violence. This pattern isn't used in all societies: in Saudi Arabia, for instance, the crown passes to the monarch's next eldest brother. The preference for a male successor stems from the time when the king's most important role was as a military leader. If all of the siblings had killed one another, then the throne passed to the nearest relative—or the deadliest fighter.

When Edward IV married Elizabeth Woodville in 1464, she was a widow with two sons. She was called "the most beautiful woman in the Island of Britain."

the throne when he was less than a year old, and the country had fallen into chaos and instability. Richard was much more experienced than his young nephew and may have felt that by taking the throne, he was doing what was best for England.

And what happened to Edward V and his brother, confined in the Tower of London? They definitely died—the boys were never seen again after the summer of 1483. Richard always remained silent about their fate. Historians assume the two boys were murdered, but no one knows for certain, or who did it. Many people suspected Richard, and over time he became notorious for the murders.

But why would he kill them, especially when he knew their deaths would immediately be blamed on him? Richard had nothing to gain by the boys' deaths—they'd already been declared illegitimate. Besides, there were many more subtle ways their uncle could have gotten rid of them if he'd wanted to. For instance, the princes could have become "ill," then died, and been buried with great honors. Today, most historians agree that Richard was not the princes' murderer.

WHO DONE IT?

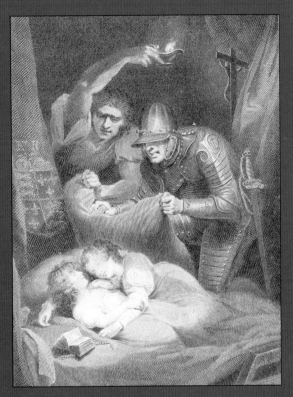

To this day, no one has solved the mystery of the deaths of the two young boys who've become known as the Princes in the Tower. If Richard III didn't murder them, who did? So many people wanted the princes dead, it's almost surprising they lasted as long as they did. One of the many possible murderers is Henry Tudor of the House of Lancaster, who ruled after Richard as Henry VII. The boys could have posed a challenge to his right to the throne. Henry's mother and father also have been accused of the double murder. As well, there are dukes who may have felt they could claim the throne if only the princes were out of the way. Even Lord Thomas Stanley, who would later betray Richard, is a suspect.

It's also possible the princes were not murdered at all. Five hundred years ago, many children died before reaching adulthood. Perhaps the princes died of a fatal disease or illness.

Almost 200 years after the boys are thought to have died, workmen at the Tower of London dug up a box containing two small human skeletons. It was decided these were the two princes, so the skeletons were buried in Westminster Abbey, alongside the bodies of many of England's monarchs. But that didn't lay to rest the rumors and stories. Because the Princes in the Tower were so young and innocent when they disappeared, they still capture the public's sympathy and imagination.

The boys were probably still alive on July 6, 1483, when Richard was crowned Richard III, king of England. Because of his experience in the north of the country, he was a fair and clever ruler. He tried to provide justice for all of his subjects, including the poor. The first laws written completely in English were passed during his reign. Up to that point Latin had also been used, an ancient language many commoners didn't understand.

BAD REP

Ask people what they know about Richard III and most will tell you he was a hunchback who killed his nephews. But experts now say that both of those things are probably untrue. How did these stories become accepted as facts?

The main history about Richard wasn't published until after his death. It was written by Sir Thomas More, who was trying to please the British monarch at the time. That king was descended from Richard's enemy, Henry VII, so More made sure that Richard appeared especially vile.

But the person probably most responsible for the world's bad opinion of this king is the famous playwright William Shakespeare. His play *Richard III* paints Richard as a vengeful villain who will stop at nothing to succeed.

Why did Shakespeare make Richard such a despicable character? For one thing, he used More's text as his main source of information. Secondly, by the time Shakespeare wrote the play, in the late 1500s, Elizabeth I was queen of England. She was a granddaughter of Henry VII, who had taken the throne from Richard III. Shakespeare figured that blackening Richard's name would improve his own status with the queen. In addition, Shakespeare was trying to write an entertaining play, not necessarily one that was historically accurate. Audiences are fascinated by a character who is unrelentingly evil—and most actors prefer playing a villain rather than a saint.

Why do so many people think that Richard had a hunch-back? Again, because of Shakespeare. In the playwright's time it was believed that a person with such an abnormality also had an abnormal mind. Giving a character a hunchback immediately signaled to the audience that he was a villain. But Richard was also a warrior, who would have worn as much as 36 kilograms (80 pounds) of armor into battle—impossible if he'd been hunchbacked.

Today, groups such as the Richard III Society try to convince people to take another look at Richard's story and judge for themselves the truth about the monarch.

Richard introduced the bail system to ensure that people accused of a crime would not be imprisoned until they could be tried in court. It's still used in England and North America today. As well, to protect both buyers and sellers, Richard made weights and measurements standard across the land. He also abolished the practice of people buying jobs or positions. Now such placements had to be earned.

Spreading justice to all classes, rich and poor, was important to Richard. He had a genuine concern for the welfare of his citizens. Some of the aristocracy who'd enjoyed privileges simply because of their wealth didn't take kindly to the new laws. As well, people in the south of England said that Richard favored people in the north. It wasn't long before the country was caught up in the turbulence of rebellion again.

The initial uprisings were put down by Richard, but soon personal events were taking his attention. His only son, Edward, died in April 1484; his wife, less than a year later. It's likely they both died of tuberculosis, a lung disease, but of course there were those who said Richard was guilty. However, Richard seemed genuinely stricken by their deaths. It was reported that after they died he "was never quiet in his mind, never thought himself secure, his hand ever on his dagger. He took ill rest at night."

By now, Richard's enemies were uniting to support Henry Tudor, the Lancastrian claimant to the throne. The two sides confronted each other at Bosworth Field, in the middle of England, on August 22, 1485. Richard's forces formed a single line, facing Henry's troops across the field. Richard had the better position, at the top of a hill, but didn't have the number of soldiers he'd expected. When he looked out on the battlefield, he saw some of his expected allies arranged to the south and north, completing the square. They were waiting to see who—Richard or Henry—looked most successful and would then join the battle on the winning side.

POISONED PLOTS

People whispered that Richard had poisoned his wife. Poison was a weapon often used by assassins. It became known as "the women's weapon": it was the means of murder often chosen by females because it didn't require physical strength. Poisoning was such a threat that most monarchs had their food tasted before they ate.

MULTI-PURPOSE PALACE

When Richard III was king of England, the Tower of London was used primarily as a palace and a royal refuge during rebellions. However, noble-born prisoners were kept there as early as 1100. The first execution took place in the infamous Tower in 1483, during Richard III's reign, but it was only later that the Tower became known as a place of beheadings.

There are 20 towers in the Tower of London and their function seems to change through time. The White Tower (the central tower) was the one in which prisoners were kept. Richard's young prince nephews were likely kept in the White Tower, since their bones were later found here, but this is also where the royal family lived in medieval times. Elizabeth I was later imprisoned in the Bell Tower.

Anticipating that something like this might happen, Richard had kidnapped one of the waiting leaders' sons. Richard had the boy brought to the top of the hill where his father, Lord Stanley, could see him. Richard then sent the treacherous lord the message that his son would be executed unless Lord Stanley ordered his troops to join the king's army. The lord coolly replied that he had more sons and that his army was staying just where it was. Richard was angry but later released the son unharmed.

The savage battle raged, bloody and deadly, for two long hours. When it became clear that Lord Stanley and the others were not going to join Richard's side, the king's advisers begged him to retreat. "God forbid that I yield one foot," retorted Richard furiously. "This day I will perish as king or have the victory."

Rashly, Richard still felt he could win if he could just kill Henry Tudor. He figured that with Henry dead, his forces would have no reason to keep fighting. Richard slammed his crown on his head over his armor so that everyone would know the king was entering battle. Accompanied by a small group of loyal supporters, he thundered down the hill toward the enemy.

The attackers almost reached Henry, but Lord Stanley chose that moment to bring in his forces on Henry's side. Richard's men were suddenly outnumbered, and Richard was knocked off his horse. The crown had made Richard an easy target for his enemies. The king continued to fight bravely but was overpowered and killed. History records that it was the double-crossing Lord Stanley who found

Richard's crown on the field, for which he was given the honor of crowning Henry VII the new king of England.

At the age of just 32, Richard was dead. His body was simply dumped in a heap with other dead soldiers. When it was discovered in the pile, the corpse was draped over the back of a horse

At the Battle of Bosworth Field, Richard III became the last king of England to die in battle.

47

AND DON'T DO IT AGAIN!

Long ago, if a royal murderer was caught and sentenced to death, the best end he or she could hope for was beheading. This was the usual punishment for a major crime, such as treason, but it was generally saved for rich, important, or special criminals.

Hanging was the main form of execution for many crimes, including poaching royal deer or conspiracy. Death by hanging took a long time and was very painful—especially if the criminal's heart was pulled out while he or she was still alive. The executioner simply plunged his hand into the criminal's body. After that, the body was taken down and the head was cut off and impaled on a pole as a warning to anyone who was considering a life in crime.

and carried to the nearby town of Leicester. Some people say that it was paraded naked through the streets as a final humiliation and to show the public that Richard really was dead. No one knows for sure what happened to the body after that.

Richard had reigned for only two years, two months, and two days but remains one of the most talked-about monarchs in English history. For years after his death it was accepted that he was an evil murderer who got what he deserved at Bosworth Field. Now experts are re-examining his life and debating his true legacy.

Did Richard really execute all those who stood between him and the throne of England, or has he become infamous for murders he never committed? Why would Richard murder his brother's children, especially when their deaths had no effect on his right to England's throne? Richard was a courageous royal but was impetuous and unlucky—in his personal life, in battle, and perhaps in legend.

WHAT HAPPENED WHEN?

KING	REIGN	HOW HE DIED
Henry VI	1422–1461, 1470–1471	Murdered
Edward IV (Richard III's brother)	1461–1470, 1471–1483	Illness
Richard III	1483–1485	In battle
Henry VII	1485–1509	Illness

Mary I, Elizabeth I, and Mary, Queen of Scots

Killing Cousins

Elizabeth's

heart sank when the men came for her. Fear clutched at her throat. She knew they were taking her to the Tower of London on charges of treason against England's Queen Mary, her half-sister. Elizabeth knew that many people who entered the dreaded gates of the Tower never exited. The scared young royal, just 20 years old, shivered as she thought of her mother, Anne Boleyn, who had been beheaded in the Tower 18 years earlier, in 1536.

Queen Mary insisted that Elizabeth be taken to the Tower by river because she feared some of Elizabeth's supporters might attempt a rescue if she traveled by land. Perhaps Mary also wanted Elizabeth to see what happened to traitors. The heads of men who had plotted against Mary rested on sharp spikes lining the river. Elizabeth gazed in horror at the grisly sight. Was she going to share their wretched fate? As icy rain soaked her, she shook with cold and fear.

Large, burly men in full armor escorted the slim, pale woman into the Tower. Elizabeth tried to stay calm by reminding herself that she hadn't done anything wrong. She wasn't involved in the plot to oust Mary. But if Mary could prove she even knew about the scheme, Elizabeth would not leave the Tower alive.

As Elizabeth was marched through Traitor's Gate into the Tower, her courage failed her, and she sank down on the cold, wet stone. When the guards tried to force her to her feet, Elizabeth said, "Better sitting here, than in a worse place! For, God knoweth! I know not whither you will bring me!" But soon Elizabeth was locked in a cell, isolated from the Tower's other prisoners, to await her fate at Mary's hands.

Why did Queen Mary hate Elizabeth, her half-sister, so much? It all started with their father, Henry VIII. He had married Mary's mother, Catherine, in 1509. Seven years later, Mary was born. While Henry was proud of his daughter, he desperately wanted a son to inherit his throne. It seemed unlikely that Catherine would provide him with a male heir. Besides, he'd fallen in love with a lady-in-waiting in the court, Anne Boleyn.

Elizabeth was forced to enter the Tower of London through the Traitor's Gate (above). She knew her mother had also entered the Tower this way—and had ended up dead.

Henry VIII (1491–1547)

King 1509–1547

WIVES	CHILDREN
Catherine of Aragon (1485–1536) Henry's wife 1509 to 1533 (Divorced)	**Mary I (1516–1558)** Queen 1553–1558
Anne Boleyn (about 1501–1536) Henry's wife 1533 to 1536 (Beheaded)	**Elizabeth I (1533–1603)** Queen 1558–1603
Jane Seymour (about 1508–1537) Henry's wife 1536 to 1537 (Died)	**Edward VI (1537–1553)** King 1547–1553
Anne of Cleves (1515–1557) Henry's wife in 1540 (Divorced)	
Kathryn Howard (about 1523–1542) Henry's wife 1540 to 1542 (Beheaded)	
Katherine Parr (about 1512–1548) Henry's wife 1543 to 1547 (Outlived Henry)	

(Only children included are those who lived past infancy.)

However, Henry was a Roman Catholic, and he needed permission from the Pope, the head of the Catholic Church, if he wanted to remarry. Catherine had many powerful Catholic friends and relatives, so Henry knew he was unlikely to obtain that permission.

When the Pope refused to cancel Henry's first marriage, the king broke away from Catholicism. He declared himself head of the English Church. His followers became part of the religious movement known as Protestantism. Henry caused further turmoil when he began to give Protestants increasing power in his government. In the eyes of Roman Catholics, Henry was no longer king of England, so citizens were not required to obey him.

DANGEROUS MAGIC

When Henry VIII grew tired of Elizabeth's mother, Anne Boleyn, he claimed she was a witch who'd enchanted him into falling in love with her. Back then, being taller than usual, having moles or warts, or having power (in Anne's case, royal power) were enough to brand a woman as a witch. Unfortunately for Anne, she had all three. Some people are still fascinated by the historical depictions of Anne: her portrait hangs in Hogwarts School in the movie *Harry Potter and the Sorcerer's Stone.*

Mary (far right) was the first queen in England, not counting Jane Grey, in more than 400 years. Some people think the nursery rhyme "Mary, Mary, Quite Contrary" is based on her life.

Anne and Henry were married in 1533. Later that year, Elizabeth was born. It had been difficult enough for Mary when her father married for the second time. Mary's mother had been banished and Mary was not allowed to visit her. Although Mary was Henry's oldest child, anyone associated with Mary's mother was now out of favor, and that included Mary. With Elizabeth's birth, Mary was demoted from Princess Mary to Lady Mary. Mary's importance and power were greatly diminished. What would happen to her?

Things soon became even more uncertain. Though Henry was pleased with his new daughter, Elizabeth, who was red-haired as he was, he still wanted a son. When Anne didn't give him one, he wanted another wife. Henry found a reason to accuse Anne of treason and soon had her beheaded.

Henry next married Jane Seymour, who gave him the son, Edward, that he desired. Now it was Elizabeth's turn to be demoted to merely Lady Elizabeth. Over the years, Henry took three additional wives but had no more children. When Henry died in 1547, Edward became king of England—even though he was only nine years old.

Edward's days were numbered, however. He developed tuberculosis and died when he was just 15. As Edward lay dying, his advisers had convinced him to ignore his half-sisters, Mary and Elizabeth, and name Lady Jane Grey, a distant relative, next in line for the throne. Other groups in England fought Jane's allies, and she was queen for only nine days before she was beheaded. The 1500s were a dangerous time to be of royal blood.

Who became England's monarch after Jane? Mary had enough supporters that they succeeded in their fight to put her on the throne. Still there was no peace for England. Like her mother, Mary was a strong Roman Catholic. She was determined to make England Catholic again. As more and more Protestants were burned at the stake or killed in other gruesome ways, she became known as Bloody Mary.

SHARP CHOICE

When Anne Boleyn, Elizabeth's mother, was sentenced to be beheaded, it was arranged that she be killed with a French sword. These swords were sharper than the traditional English axe, making beheading faster and less painful. Elizabeth knew about her mother's execution, and she planned to ask for the same favor if her half-sister Mary chose to behead her.

One of the chief reasons Mary still hated Elizabeth was that she suspected the younger woman was Protestant even though Elizabeth was careful to hide her beliefs. Mary felt she had to crush all who disagreed with her on any issue, especially religion, and Elizabeth was high on her list. But what really infuriated Mary was that if she died without having any children, Elizabeth would take over as queen, and England would probably become Protestant again.

Before Mary could have children, she had to find a husband. When she saw a portrait of a handsome young Spanish prince, she immediately fell in love with him. Soon she announced her plans to marry Prince Philip, to the horror of many English people— even her supporters. Back in the 1500s, when a queen married, her husband took over ruling her country. A foreigner govern us, thought the English? Never! This was why a group of nobles had engineered the plot against Queen Mary that resulted in Elizabeth being hauled off to the Tower of London. If Mary's supporters could prove that Elizabeth knew about the plot, Mary could have her half-sister beheaded and be rid of her forever.

Elizabeth was questioned intently about the plot against Mary. Despite furiously denying all accusations, Elizabeth still feared that every day could be her last. She knew there were staff in the Tower who wouldn't wait for an official order for her execution. They might poison her food or find some other way to make her "disappear." As often as possible, Elizabeth had her own servants prepare and deliver her food, but sometimes the guards refused to let in her people. Elizabeth was powerless and desperately afraid.

More than two months after she'd been imprisoned, Elizabeth was suddenly ordered to prepare to travel. Was she being sent somewhere to be beheaded? Elizabeth was so unnerved that she begged to stay in the Tower. But Mary hadn't been able to find a good enough reason to execute her half-sister and realized she couldn't keep her in the Tower forever. Mary

arranged for Elizabeth to be taken downriver where she'd be kept in a chilly, miserable house some distance from London. Crowds cheered as Elizabeth sailed by, delighted to see she'd been released. The bells in churches joyfully rang out—until the bell-ringers were punished. Elizabeth was alive and popular, but she would remain a prisoner for about another year.

Meanwhile, Mary's unpopularity increased when she went ahead with her plans to marry Prince Philip of Spain. The queen also imposed heavy new taxes on her subjects and continued to burn non-Catholics. In February 1555, 300 people were burned at the stake because they were, or were believed to be, Protestants. The country grew tired and repulsed by so much violence. Increasingly, Protestants looked to Elizabeth to save them.

As Mary became less and less popular with her subjects, they increasingly rallied behind Elizabeth (above). Their love for the younger woman made Mary furious.

Within the illustration: On afoze Onafoze

Hold vp your torches for dropping.

Salue festa dies

Mary went to great lengths to try to abolish Protestantism in England. For instance, Martin Bucer was a leading Protestant who died in 1551, before Mary became queen. Six years later, when Mary was on the throne, she gave orders for Bucer's tomb to be demolished and his body was burned, as shown here.

When a comet blazed through the skies in the summer of 1558, Protestants were filled with fresh hope. After all, people believed that such a sign predicted the death of a ruler. Was it just coincidence that in the fall Mary became ill? Mary realized that she was dying and unhappily sent word to Elizabeth that she would be the next monarch. Elizabeth's response couldn't help but exasperate Mary: "…there is no reason why I should thank her for her intention to give me the crown of this kingdom. For she has neither the power of bestowing it upon me, nor can I lawfully be deprived of it, since it is my peculiar and hereditary right."

After reading this haughty note, Mary may have regretted her decision to allow Elizabeth to succeed her, but it was too late. Mary died of cancer in November, and Elizabeth became queen.

It was tradition that an English monarch spent the night before he or she was crowned in the Tower of London. It must have brought back terrifying memories for the young queen. However, Elizabeth's experience had taught her confidence, discipline, and patience. She would need all of these qualities and a lot of cunning to remain on the throne—and to stay alive.

Elizabeth inherited a country that was impoverished and had become a minor power in Europe. The struggle for the throne wasn't over yet, but Elizabeth was a shrewd politician. Although she was Protestant, as Mary had suspected, she tried to find compromises between the two religious groups in her country. When agreements weren't possible, her opponents were locked in the Tower of London. The ancient prison saw one of its busiest periods when Elizabeth I was on the throne.

Because of the common people's warm response to Elizabeth when she'd been released from the Tower, she loved and respected her subjects. Not only was she kind and sympathetic to them, she knew how to maintain her influence by how she chose to dress, by her speech, and other actions. When some village women prepared a feast for Elizabeth, she ate the food without first having a food taster test it for poison. Her subjects loved her for trusting them. Elizabeth's advisers often felt she was indecisive, but avoiding rash decisions worked to her advantage.

Generally, the country was happy with their queen. But some people, especially Elizabeth's nobles, protested against being ruled by an unmarried woman. There were those who found it unthinkable that a woman would attempt to rule a country on her own without a man to guide and protect her. It was also believed in the 1500s that a woman who remained unmarried was probably very mentally unstable.

But whom could Elizabeth marry? She'd seen what happened to Mary's popularity when she'd married a foreigner. A foreign royal husband might also drain all of England's money to protect his own country against enemies. Or he might see

THE TOWER OF LONDON

Most people today think of the Tower of London as a prison and execution site. However, at one time it was tradition for English monarchs to live there until they were crowned.

There are several towers within the Tower of London. But more infamous than the towers is the Tower Green, an area in the enclosure's lawn. Here high-born people, including Anne Boleyn, were privately executed. Most people were executed outside on Tower Hill, with huge crowds watching.

Today if you visit the Tower, you may see the ghost of Anne Boleyn. Watch for ravens too. There's a legend that if the ravens ever leave the Tower of London, a horrible fate awaits England. So attendants trim the ravens' flight feathers so the birds can't fly away.

Elizabeth's country as very unimportant relative to his own. The new queen loved England too much to accept that.

Elizabeth realized it could be even more dangerous to marry one of her own subjects. That would cause rivalries in her court and might result in a threat to her throne. Besides, Elizabeth was proud of her royal blood and felt that marrying a commoner was beneath her.

Elizabeth also knew that marrying would cost her greatly. All of the properties and income she'd inherited from her father were hers only until she took a husband. Marriage would also mean less independence—having been imprisoned already, she didn't want to lose her new freedom.

Elizabeth allowed various princes to court her and had many suitors. Two of the most famous were Robert Dudley (1st Earl of Leicester) and his stepson, Robert Devereux (2nd Earl of Essex), who was more than 30 years younger than the queen. Dudley was married for the early part of Elizabeth's reign, but his wife fell down a flight of stairs and died in mysterious circumstances. Some people thought Dudley may have arranged the accident so he could marry the queen and that Elizabeth even knew about the plot. However, first Dudley and then Devereux eventually fell from Elizabeth's favor.

The queen's advisers not only tried to get her to marry but also begged her to declare a successor. While she kept promising she would, it wouldn't be until very late in her life that she would make her choice known. Elizabeth knew the dangers of announcing an heir. Opponents might rally around the future ruler and conspire to rebel against her. Since so many of her subjects and counselors felt a woman was incapable of ruling the country, she worried that conspirators would help a male successor overthrow her or force her to abdicate.

It's also possible that Elizabeth equated marriage with death, thanks to her father's example. Elizabeth's mother had been beheaded, as had another of Henry's six wives. Her half-brother

POPULAR QUEEN

Elizabeth I was popular when she was alive, and she still is. In a 2002 poll, British people ranked her seventh in a list of the top 100 Britons ever, royal or common. That was ahead of any other British ruler. In 2005, British historians and other experts ranked her England's best monarch ever.

There have been more movies made about Elizabeth than about any other monarch—king or queen. Both she and her cousin Mary, Queen of Scots have had operas, plays, and many books written about them. Elizabeth's half-sister, Bloody Mary, has had a number of books written about her but has never inspired the same interest as her queenly relatives.

Mary, Queen of Scots is one of the most famous Scottish monarchs, because of her event-filled and tragic life. Her father was bitterly disappointed when she was born that she wasn't a boy. He predicted that Mary would be the last of their family to reign in Scotland but he was wrong.

Edward's mother had died soon after giving birth to him. Death caused by childbirth was a common end for women in Elizabeth's time, so perhaps she was scared to have children. Whatever the reason, Elizabeth stayed single all her life and never had children.

Meanwhile, another Mary was about to make Elizabeth's life difficult. The queen's new enemy was her cousin Mary Stuart, also known as Mary, Queen of Scots. Mary was eight years younger than Elizabeth and had become queen of Scotland after the death of her father, when

she was just a baby. From the moment Mary was born, she didn't fit in. Her father and her country didn't want a princess, they wanted a prince.

When Mary was five, her mother, who was born in France, had sent Mary to France to be raised by the royal family there. Because Mary was so young, her mother ruled in Scotland during that time. In 1558, Mary married François, the heir to the throne of France. When he was crowned king of France about a year later, Mary became queen of France as well as of Scotland. François died at the end of 1560, however. When his brother ascended to France's throne, Mary was no longer queen there, so she returned to Scotland.

Mary's long stay in France had made her a stranger to the Scottish people. And religion affected this Mary's life too—by returning to Scotland, she became a Catholic ruler in a Protestant country. She was hated by many of her subjects.

This Mary would soon become a problem for Queen Elizabeth because many Roman Catholics in England felt Mary was the true queen of their country. Catholics in England didn't recognize Henry VIII's marriage to Anne Boleyn as legal, so they saw Elizabeth as illegitimate. And Mary was next in line to England's throne. When Mary grew up, plots were hatched to put her on Elizabeth's throne—and most of them involved murdering Elizabeth.

Mary Queen of Scots (1542-1587)
Queen 1542–1567

HUSBANDS	CHILD
François II of France (1544–1560) Mary's husband 1558 to 1560	
Lord Darnley (1545–1567) Mary's husband 1565 to 1567	**James (1566–1625)** King of Scotland 1567–1625 King of England 1603–1625
4th Earl of Bothwell (about 1535–1578) Mary's husband 1567 to 1578	

Mary and Elizabeth pretended to be friendly, but the two never really got along. Like her followers, Mary believed she was the true queen of England, and she sometimes called herself that. Elizabeth understood that Mary could be a threat, so she handled her cousin with care. The two women were very different and couldn't understand each other. Unlike Elizabeth, who drove her counselors crazy because she was slow to make a decision, impetuous Mary had no trouble rashly jumping into action, no matter how dangerous the situation.

In 1565, Mary married Lord Darnley, a cousin who also had some claim to the English throne. Elizabeth felt herself to be in danger, especially when it was discovered that Darnley's mother had secretly plotted to replace Elizabeth with her son and his wife. All Elizabeth could do was keep a careful eye on the pair and be grateful that Mary hadn't married a rich, powerful prince with the money to back a Scottish war against England.

Although the Scottish queen had married Darnley for love—as well as possibly a bid for Elizabeth's throne—she was soon unhappy with her choice. Darnley was jealous and arrogant, and he drank too much. Mary spent more and more time with one of her staff, David Rizzio. One night while Rizzio, a skilled musician, was playing for Mary and some of her staff, Darnley and a group of lords barged into the room. Rizzio tried to grab hold of the queen, but the men dragged him away and stabbed him—some reports say as many as 57 times—just outside the door.

Mary was devastated. Although a son, James, was born to Mary and Darnley about three months later, their life together was miserable. Mary began to rely on one of her noblemen, the 4th Earl of Bothwell. She looked for ways to end her marriage, no matter what the cost.

Darnley became very sick and rested in a house outside the palace, with Mary visiting him often. People began to wonder if their relationship was improving. But in February 1567, Darnley's house was bombed, and though he was found dead, it was not

"NO MORE TEARS NOW; I WILL THINK ABOUT REVENGE."

—MARY, QUEEN OF SCOTS

DARK DISMAL END

What happened to Mary's third husband, Bothwell? He escaped to Scandinavia, where he hoped to gather an army and put Mary back on her throne. But instead he was imprisoned for not having the proper papers and for likely being involved in the death of Lord Darnley.

Bothwell escaped from his prison cell but was recaptured and thrown into a notorious prison in Denmark. Bothwell was chained by leg irons to a post in the center of a cold, damp, windowless room, but his chain was so short that he could barely walk halfway around the post. After 10 years, he eventually died in the miserable hole. Mary probably never knew what happened to him.

because of the explosion—he'd been strangled. There was no doubt he'd been murdered.

Bothwell was tried for the crime but found innocent. Shortly afterwards, Mary was kidnapped—possibly willingly—by Bothwell and his men. On May 15, 1567, he and the queen were wed. Even Mary's strongest supporters were shocked when she married the man suspected of killing her husband. Although there was continual unrest in Scotland, never before had Mary experienced real hatred from her people. She finally realized how much many of her subjects disliked her.

Scottish nobles gathered troops to fight the newlyweds. Before the two sides could battle, Mary surrendered, and Bothwell fled the country. The queen was imprisoned and forced to give up her throne to her one-year-old son. Until now, Elizabeth had seemed friendly in her correspondence with Mary. When Mary wrote to her cousin asking for rescue, she truly believed Elizabeth would help her. But England's queen was too careful to act so impulsively. Besides, Elizabeth's goodwill toward Mary was just a front to keep their two countries at peace.

Mary soon realized her cousin probably would not help her. But Mary had a rare ability to find supporters and helpers, even among her jailers. With their assistance, Mary escaped from her confinement on May 2, 1568, and managed to raise an army. She dreamed of regaining her throne—and maybe taking Elizabeth's. But Mary often rashly ignored her best advisers. It wasn't long before a group of Scotland's noblemen defeated Mary's troops. The queen was on the run. She felt she had no choice but to escape to England, where she was quickly captured by English forces and held in a castle in northwest England. It's hard to believe, but Mary still thought Elizabeth might help her—perhaps she felt that because Elizabeth was a queen, and had herself once been wrongly imprisoned, she would come to Mary's aid.

As much as Elizabeth had to admire Mary's courage and tenacity, England's queen was exasperated by her cousin. Mary's power and influence jeopardized peace in England. Elizabeth was even more frightened by how Mary's own nobles had turned on her. Would Elizabeth's lords do the same to her? Many of Elizabeth's advisers argued that she should execute Mary, but England's queen refused. She would not kill her cousin and fellow ruler. Nor would Elizabeth release Mary so that her cousin's enemies could assassinate her. Perhaps Mary also reminded Elizabeth of her own mother—both women had been brought up in France, both had flirtatious personalities, and both were queens. No matter what Elizabeth's reasons, none of her advisers were sympathetic to Elizabeth's inaction.

Mary owed her life to Elizabeth, but the Scottish queen still conspired to regain her throne—and to take Elizabeth's too! Why did Mary keep trying to escape her imprisonment despite repeated failures? Like most prisoners, her days were mind-numbingly repetitive and boring. To stay sane, Mary plotted almost impossible escapes that seemed pointless to other people.

Mary got fresh hope in 1570 when she received news that her only sibling, her illegitimate half-brother James, had been assassinated. True, if he could be murdered, Mary easily could too. But she preferred to dream that his death meant that she'd be called home to Scotland now that another of her enemies was dead. As the years passed and nothing happened, Mary suggested to her secret supporters that if she couldn't rule over her former country alone, she could rule it with her son, James. But Mary was as much of a nuisance to her son as she was to Elizabeth. James had nothing to gain by agreeing to share his throne with his mother, and nothing came of this plan.

Mary's hopes of escape and regaining her power increased as she learned of Elizabeth's dithering over executing an English noble who had plotted against her. The exiled queen took this to mean that Elizabeth didn't have the courage to put high-born traitors to death. Elizabeth's words seemed to prove this. When members of parliament encouraged her to get rid of Mary

"What will my enemies not say, that for the safety of her life a maiden queen could be content to spill the blood even of her own kinswoman?"

—ELIZABETH I, 1586

GUN~ POWDER PLOT

Murder between Catholics and Protestants didn't end with Elizabeth's death. James I had been brought up Protestant (like most Scots) and faced many attempts on his life by Catholic groups, including the most famous one, the Gunpowder Plot, on November 5, 1605.

Guy Fawkes, an explosives expert, hid 817 kilograms (1800 pounds) of gunpowder in the vaults below the Houses of Parliament in London. Modern tests have determined that this gunpowder had enough explosive power to kill everyone in the Houses of Parliament as well as blow out all windows within a huge area around the site. But a tip led to the discovery of the gunpowder— and Fawkes's arrest.

On November 5 each year, people in England celebrate the discovery of the plot on Guy Fawkes Night. Some people think the word *guy*, meaning a person, comes from his name.

permanently, she replied, "Shall I put to death the bird that, to escape the hawk, has fled to my feet for protection? Honour and conscience forbid."

But Mary shouldn't have been too smug. Her cousin's spies intercepted a letter from Mary, written at a castle in the middle of England, and when they translated the code, Elizabeth angrily read, "There is yet a strong party in my favour, and lords who favour my cause, of whom although certain ones are prisoners, the Queen of England would not dare touch their lives." It wasn't conclusive evidence of a plot, but Elizabeth was furious to learn that Mary felt the English queen wouldn't take action, no matter what treasonous plots were planned. Elizabeth might not make a move without carefully thinking through the consequences, but she was not as weak as Mary thought.

By 1586, Elizabeth could no long ignore Mary's plotting. The queen's spies had discovered another scheme to release Mary from her imprisonment, then kill Elizabeth. This time there was definite proof of Mary's involvement. Elizabeth was furious as well as hurt, since she had protected her cousin's life for so long.

Mary was found guilty of treason against the queen. Even then, Elizabeth couldn't bring herself at first to sign Mary's death warrant. No crowned queen had ever been executed before. Elizabeth tried to convince Mary's jailer to kill her quietly, but he refused. When Elizabeth eventually put her signature to the order for Mary's beheading, her counselors rushed to carry out the order before she could change her mind.

On February 8, 1587, Mary entered the great hall of the castle that had been her final prison. She was dressed in black from head to toe. As she paused at the foot of the stairs leading to the stage where she would be beheaded, her jailer, who had refused Elizabeth's request to kill Mary, offered the doomed woman his hand. "I thank you, sir," she said quietly. "This is the last trouble I shall ever give you."

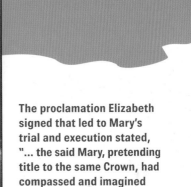

The proclamation Elizabeth signed that led to Mary's trial and execution stated, "... the said Mary, pretending title to the same Crown, had compassed and imagined within the same realm divers things tending to the hurt, death and destruction of our royal person ..." It was all true but Elizabeth still hated taking such drastic action.

According to tradition, two of Mary's servants then helped her remove her outer dress. The crowd gasped when Mary's bright red petticoat and bodice were revealed. Mary had chosen the color carefully—red was the color of martyrdom in the Catholic Church. Obviously, Mary felt she was a martyr for her religion. Bravely, she placed her head on the executioner's block.

The execution was cruel and painful to watch. It took three blows to finally complete the job. The legend sprang up that Mary's execution had been deliberately painful to punish her for her treasonous plotting. The story is also told that after the beheading, when the executioner picked up the severed head by the hair, he discovered that Mary was wearing a wig. The people gathered about were shocked again when Mary's little Skye terrier rushed out from under the dead queen's skirts. The poor little dog didn't survive for long after the trauma of its mistress's death.

When Elizabeth heard of Mary's execution, she claimed to be shocked and upset. But she also must have been relieved. The English queen had kept Mary in captivity in various

When Mary removed her black outer gown before her execution, she gave the executioner a small smile and said, "Never have I had such assistants to disrobe me, and never have I put off my clothes before such a company."

castles around England for about 19 years—almost half of Mary's life. After Mary left Scotland in 1568, she never returned to the country where she'd been born.

Elizabeth continued on her throne for more than 15 years, far outliving the two Marys who had caused her so much anguish. Perhaps it was because all of this uncertainty was over that the last years of her life were a golden age for England. In 1603, as she lay dying (likely of old age), Elizabeth finally named Mary, Queen of Scots's son, James, king of England. (He was already king of Scotland.) James was Protestant, so both Bloody Mary's and Mary, Queen of Scots's desire for Catholic countries had died with them.

Mary, Queen of Scots and Elizabeth had such influence on each other's lives that it's hard to believe that the two women never met. Even more amazing is that now they are buried just 9 meters (30 feet) from each other in London's Westminster Abbey.

Louis XVI and Marie Antoinette

Too Little, Too Late

Maria Antonia

lay back in her carriage, crying as though her heart would break. She was just 14 and would never again see her mother or her home in Vienna, Austria. The young arch-duchess was on her way to France, to marry Louis-Auguste, who would one day be the king of France. But right now Maria Antonia wasn't queen of France, she was just a homesick girl, scared of life in a faraway country. She'd had to be carried half-fainting to her carriage. Perhaps the young royal would have been even more overcome if she'd had any idea what fate had in store for her.

Marriage to such an important royal as Louis would not have originally been predicted for someone such as Maria Antonia. In fact, from the day she was born, in 1755, her future prospects seemed almost dire. She was born on November 2, known as the Day of the Dead and a very solemn day, not one to celebrate. On the same day, her godparents' country, Portugal, was devastated by an earthquake that killed 30,000.

Usually when a baby was born in Maria Antonia's family, the father, Emperor Francis I, threw a great public banquet. But for some unknown reason, he didn't on this occasion. When he asked a soothsayer about the baby's horoscope, the forecaster stated her life would be difficult, then turned pale and would say no more. Her father wondered what was ahead for this poor child.

Maria Antonia's childhood did almost nothing to prepare her for life as a queen in turbulent times and in a foreign country. She saw little of her mother, who focused less on her many children—she had 16, although only 10 lived to be adults—and more on dictating letters, checking files, and signing documents. When her doctor suggested she should rest with her family after the birth of Maria Antonia, the 15th child, Maria Theresa said, "My subjects are my first children. My first care must be for them; the others must come after." No wonder Maria Antonia and her siblings feared and respected their strong-minded

Maria Antonia (far right) would become one of the most important trendsetters of her time. She would wear hairstyles up to 1 meter (3 feet) high. The huge gowns she, and other women copying her, wore would make females seem less passive and more important.

mother rather than loved her. When their father died before Maria Antonia's tenth birthday, she missed him terribly.

In the 1700s, royal daughters were often treated as political pawns. A young princess had no choice who would become her groom. Through marriage, she could cement a relationship with another country. When Maria Antonia was ten, it was decided by the leaders of France and Austria that the little girl would marry the future king of France, known as the dauphin, in four years. "They are born to obey and must learn to do so in good time," said Empress Maria Theresa about her daughters. She also insisted to the girls' governesses, "Never must they be allowed to be afraid, neither of thunderstorms, fire, ghosts, witches, or any other nonsense …" Maria Antonia would need that kind of courage many times during her short life.

Somehow it escaped her mother's attention that Maria Antonia hadn't received much education. The young girl found it hard to concentrate on her lessons, but then she didn't try very hard. There's a story about one teacher writing out Maria Antonia's homework in pencil and the spoiled little girl tracing over the words with a pen. She hated reading, her writing was almost impossible to decipher, and her spelling was even worse.

When Maria Antonia was 13, just a year before she was to leave for France, her mother suddenly realized that she had to do something about her daughter's lack of education. Tutors were rushed to the royal court to teach the future queen of France to speak French with a perfect accent. Of course it was vital that she sing and dance well too, as well as hunt and know the etiquette and protocol of the French court.

And something had to be done about Maria Antonia's looks! A new hairstyle helped disguise a low forehead, but her crooked teeth needed more attention. Using a system of wires known as the pelican, in three months Maria Antonia had a normal smile.

"Do so much good to the French people that they can say that I have sent them an angel," were Maria Theresa's last words to her

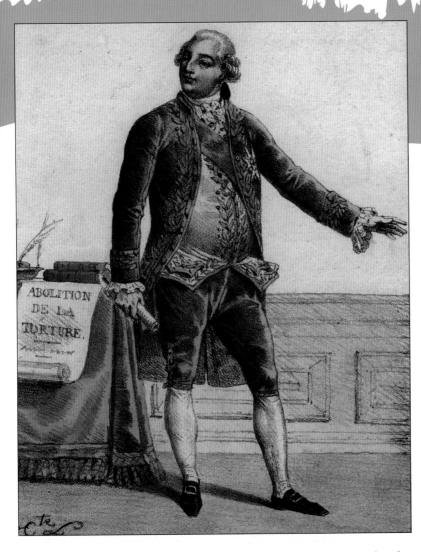

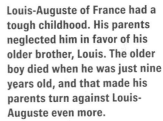

Louis-Auguste of France had a tough childhood. His parents neglected him in favor of his older brother, Louis. The older boy died when he was just nine years old, and that made his parents turn against Louis-Auguste even more.

daughter. Maria Antonia's mother needn't have worried. The French were immediately charmed by the poised and now quite beautiful young girl. One Frenchman wrote of her, "She had such a graceful word for everyone and curtsied so prettily that in a few days she delighted everyone…" This was despite the fact that as she traveled across France, she had to endure an exhausting series of fireworks, plays, parades, and other displays.

Maria Antonia met her husband for the first time on May 14, 1770, and two days later married him. France was the most powerful

The Hall of Mirrors (above) in the royal palace of Versailles is decorated with more than 350 mirrors. In the 1600s, when the hall was built, a mirror was one of the most expensive things a person could own.

country in Europe at the time. The royal palace at Versailles, just outside of Paris, where the couple was married, was the largest and most splendid on the continent. The wedding was incredibly extravagant, and Maria Antonia, now known as Marie Antoinette, wore a wedding dress studded with diamonds and pearls.

What was her new groom like? Louis wanted to be a farmer, not the king of France. The 15-year-old was interested in technology, designed and built furniture, and read many books. None of these qualities were needed in a monarch at the time. Like his new wife, Louis knew about such things as hunting, gambling, clothing, and court protocol but knew nothing of real value. He had no idea how to relate to his subjects or what was important to them.

Indeed, most of what Louis knew of being a king came from his grandfather's example. This king of France, Louis XV, was spoiled and spent his country's money extravagantly, while his subjects were starving. Louis XV let his advisers run the country and taught his grandson nothing about governing. In fact, the grandfather disliked the plump, clumsy boy, which made the younger Louis unhappy and self-conscious.

Marie Antoinette wanted to love her new husband, but he was shy and awkward. Her new aunts quarreled constantly and tried to put the teenage princess in the middle of their intrigues. They resented this newcomer and foreigner who, as wife of the dauphin, outranked them.

The etiquette of the French court mystified Marie Antoinette. She wasn't even allowed to get out of bed on her own. Then a lady-in-waiting—but only the one of the highest rank—handed Marie Antoinette her slip. One lady would put the future queen's petticoats on her, but a different lady had to tie them.

Marie Antoinette desperately wanted children, but Louis likely needed an operation before this could happen. The thought of the surgery terrified him, so Marie Antoinette sadly filled her days playing cards, dressing up in her extravagant fashions, attending parties, or going to the opera or theater.

When Louis's grandfather died of smallpox in 1774, Louis inherited a country that was close to ruin. His grandfather's extravagant ways had used up much of the nation's money, and French citizens were overtaxed and in desperate poverty. Louis XV had been one of the most unpopular French kings ever, and the citizens looked forward to change under their new king and queen. Even the brightness of Marie Antoinette's smile was celebrated, and at one concert she attended, people shouted "Long live the Queen!" for more than 15 minutes. "How fortunate we

DEADLY DISEASE

Marie Antoinette was probably the most horrified of anyone in the French court when they discovered King Louis XV was dying of smallpox. She knew more than anyone how dangerous the disease could be.

When Marie Antoinette was just 11 years old, her older sister Maria Josephina was leaving Vienna to get married. The girls' mother insisted that the bride-to-be visit the family tomb first and pay her respects to her ancestors resting there. When Maria Josephina heard this, she felt she'd received a death sentence. Her sister-in-law had just died of smallpox and had been buried in the family tomb. Maria Josephina clung to Marie Antoinette and wept bitterly, terrified that during her visit to the tomb, she'd be infected with the very contagious disease. Sadly she was right—two weeks after entering the tomb, Maria Josephina was dead from smallpox.

"LET THEM EAT CAKE!"

Marie Antoinette is infamous for saying "Let them eat cake" when told that French peasants were starving and had no bread. There's just one problem— she never said it.

The line was written by someone else, likely Marie-Thérèse (wife of Louis XIV), years before Marie Antoinette even became queen of France. Although she was very extravagant when she was young, she became more responsible and sensitive to the poor once she had children. However, many French people wanted to believe that such an unfeeling remark was typical of their foreign-born queen.

Marie Antoinette with her children Marie Thérèse Charlotte, Louis-Charles, Louis-Joseph and, in the cradle, Sophie Hélène Béatrix (far right).

are, given our rank, to have gained the love of a whole people with such ease," said Marie Antoinette happily.

But the problems in France were so great that it would have taken a very skilled politician to solve them. Instead, Louis XVI was indecisive and inexperienced. He got little help from his so-called advisers. The 3,000 aristocrats of the French royal court cared more for themselves than for their country, competing for titles, plotting against their enemies, and spreading vicious rumors and lies about one another.

The women in the court seemed determined to find fault with Marie Antoinette. It was true that the young queen yawned and giggled during long, boring royal ceremonies and gossiped with her few noble friends. Gambling became a special amusement of hers, and stories soon spread about the vast amounts of money she bet and lost. However, the French aristocrats couldn't deny that their queen was beautiful. People copied her glamorous dresses, as well as her ridiculously elaborate hairstyles.

Many people, both high-born and commoners, whispered about the fact that Louis and Marie Antoinette had no children, even hurling insults at her. In 1777, she finally convinced Louis to get the help he needed. About a year later, Marie Antoinette protested to Louis, "I have come, Sire, to complain of one of your subjects who has been so audacious as to kick me in the belly."

Marie was delighted to finally be pregnant, but giving birth would not be easy for her. It was the custom of the French court for the most important nobles in the land to attend the birth of a royal. On December 19, 1778, more than 50 aristocrats crowded into Marie Antoinette's room, some standing on furniture to get a better view. The room was so crammed that the poor queen passed out from both embarrassment and pain. Marie Antoinette declared the ridiculous ritual would never be permitted again.

Marie Antoinette gave up her gambling and parties after the birth of her daughter, Marie Thérèse Charlotte. She stopped styling her hair so wildly or wearing such ostentatious gowns.

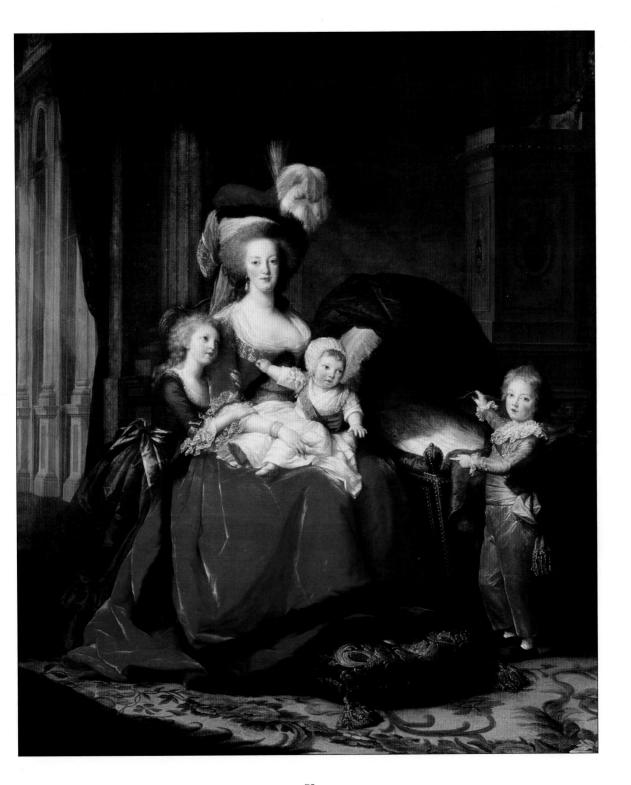

A son, Louis-Joseph Xavier François, followed in 1781, then Louis-Charles in 1785 and Sophie Hélène Béatrix in 1786. But the French couldn't forget her wild ways and the money she'd wasted when so many had been starving. They blamed Marie Antoinette more than their king because they still viewed her as a foreigner. They questioned her loyalty and resented any help Louis gave Austria, believing she must have convinced him to do it.

It seemed someone was always scheming to ruin Marie Antoinette's reputation. The worst scandal swirling around her came to be known as the "Affair of the Diamond Necklace." In 1785, one of the king's advisers, Cardinal de Rohan, was persuaded by a high-born but poor woman named Jeanne de Lamotte Valois that the queen desperately wanted to buy a beautiful diamond necklace. But, the cardinal was told, Marie Antoinette didn't want her subjects to know she was purchasing such an expensive piece of jewelry. Valois convinced the trusting cardinal that if he arranged to give the jeweler notes that supposedly came from the queen promising payment, Valois would give the jewels to the queen, who would be very grateful to the cardinal for his services.

The cardinal was anxious to improve his position in the French court, so he passed the notes to the jeweler, then gave the necklace to Valois. But she sold the jewels and kept the money. When the jeweler finally went to the queen for payment, Marie Antoinette was dumbfounded—she knew nothing about the necklace. The swindling Valois was convicted in court, but the cardinal was found innocent. Some people believed that somehow Marie Antoinette had been involved. She was humiliated, as well as shocked by how people seemed ready to despise her. She immediately set to work trying to regain the trust and love the French had shown her when she first came to the throne.

It was too late. Marie Antoinette couldn't do enough to overcome her ruined reputation. She reduced her staff, cutting jobs that were based on privilege, but this cost-cutting only

HOLD YOUR NOSE!

Although the palace of Versailles, where Louis, Marie Antoinette, and many of the French nobles lived, was beautiful and ornately decorated, it was also very smelly—there weren't enough washrooms for the thousands of people who milled about every day, so many just used the corridors!

made things more difficult for Marie Antoinette. The common people felt it was a meaningless gesture, and the nobles who lost their positions retaliated by spreading more terrible stories about the queen.

Worse events lay ahead for Louis and Marie Antoinette. Their younger daughter, Sophie, died as a baby, and two years later they lost their son Louis-Joseph to tuberculosis. Harvests of wheat and other crops had been poor, and many people were starving. The country was bankrupt.

Change was in the air. People across Europe were increasingly unhappy about being ruled by kings and queens who had not been elected and didn't seem to care about their subjects. The French citizens had heard about the rebellion against British rule that was being waged by North America's 13 colonies (today's United States) and felt encouraged in their belief that they were suffering under a useless aristocracy. Neither Louis or Marie Antoinette could understand this desire for change.

In the summer of 1789, a mob broke into the Bastille prison in downtown Paris. This prison for political criminals was a symbol for poor people of how badly they were treated by the aristocrats. The building also housed a large collection of guns and gunpowder, which the rebels carried away. The French Revolution had begun.

When tales of a lavish banquet at Versailles reached the poor of Paris in early October, starving women marched on the palace. They figured that while Louis's guards and soldiers would shoot at a throng of men, they wouldn't fire on a crowd of women. The mob met with the king, but he made them no promises for change. When the rebels found a way into the palace early the next morning, they swarmed through the halls. The foreign-born queen Marie Antoinette was their target. Three of her guards were killed as she ran for her life. Forced to move to Paris, the royal family was confined to a palace there.

STORMING THE BASTILLE

Bastille is a French word that means castle or fortress. But for most French people, it's the name of the stone building in Paris that was a focal point for the French Revolution. When the citizens of Paris took over the Bastille on July 14, 1789, they also felt they'd taken over the city—the Bastille had been a symbol of authority that had now fallen.

In the battle for the Bastille, many more rebels were killed than soldiers defending it. Still, the citizens managed to capture the leader of the garrison, whom they gruesomely beheaded with a pocketknife. They then paraded his head around on a stick.

The day the Paris mob stormed the Bastille prison has been celebrated in France ever since as a beginning of the modern French nation. Now July 14 is known as *Fête Nationale*. In English it's called Bastille Day.

This bedroom of Marie Antoinette was considered fairly plain and simple.

FOILED ESCAPE

Louis and Marie Antoinette and their children almost made it to Austria when they desperately tried to flee France in 1791. Although dressed as commoners, they were recognized when they stepped out of their carriage in Varennes, France. They'd been noticed at an earlier stop, and when they later had trouble getting fresh horses, pro-revolutionary troops seized them.

What gave them away? Some said it was the unmistakable scent of Marie's top-quality perfume. Others said her dignified posture and commanding manner were unmistakable. Or perhaps someone recognized Louis from his face on a coin. But everyone agrees: the failed flight sealed the fate of Louis and Marie Antoinette.

France seemed more stable for the next couple of years. But when one of the more moderate revolutionary leaders died, Marie Antoinette convinced Louis that they must flee to Austria. Originally, just the king and queen were going to escape, with their children to follow later. But at the last minute, Marie Antoinette refused to leave Marie Thérèse Charlotte and Louis-Charles behind. Late in the night on June 20, 1791, the royal family secretly set out. The family had to travel in a large, slow carriage and make many stops along the way to replace the tired horses.

They had almost reached safety when the carriage stopped in a small French town. Although they were dressed as commoners, Louis and Marie Antoinette were recognized and forced to return to Paris. As they retraced their flight to freedom, people lined the route to jeer at the royals. Some people reported that Marie Antoinette's legendary blonde hair had turned white overnight.

Marie Antoinette sought help from other countries. Austria, her homeland, threatened France, but that only made things worse. French citizens were convinced their queen had passed on French military secrets and had yet another reason to hate Marie Antoinette. In August 1792, rebels stormed the palace where the king and queen were living and arrested them on suspicion of treason.

Louis and Marie Antoinette were taken to a prison in an ancient, forbidding fortress in Paris. The revolutionaries abolished the monarchy, and Louis XVI was stripped of his title of king. French rebels mocked him by calling him *Louis le Dernier*—"Louis the Last." During the next month, hundreds of aristocrats were imprisoned or massacred. Marie Antoinette's best friend was killed, and parts of the woman's body were impaled on spears and marched by Marie Antoinette's prison window as the former queen wept bitterly.

Louis's torment was soon over. He was put on trial by the revolutionaries, and on January 21, 1793, the former king of France was beheaded on a guillotine. The huge crowd that gathered to watch his execution cheered wildly.

Marie Antoinette lived on for months in the filthy prison with her 8-year-old son and 14-year-old daughter. Conditions were miserable, and the children were often sick, but at least the family, what was left of it, was still together. Then the jailers moved Louis-Charles to another cell. Marie Antoinette was tortured by the sound of him crying piteously. A few weeks later, Marie Antoinette was transferred to a worse prison. She knew the end was near.

The former queen was roughly awakened one October night and taken to trial. In court, she defended herself bravely despite the sneers and insults of the prosecutor. Marie Antoinette seemed surprisingly calm and poised, but her drumming fingers gave away her fear and desperation. The outcome was never in doubt. On October 15, 1793, Marie Antoinette was found guilty of treason.

Two days later, before dawn, the former queen wrote for the last time to her children: "My God! Have pity on me! My eyes

> "I know they have come from Paris to demand my head, but I learned from my mother not to fear death and I shall await it with firmness."
>
> —MARIE ANTOINETTE, 1789

OFF WITH THEIR HEADS!

Although most people associate the guillotine, the machine that beheaded both Louis XVI and Marie Antoinette, only with the French Revolution, the deadly instrument has existed in one form or another since at least 1300. The version used in France was designed by Antoine Louis in the 1700s. At first the machine was called *louison* or *louisette,* after its creator. But later it was named for Dr. Joseph-Ignace Guillotin, a government official who had originally come up with the idea that the death penalty in France should be carried out in a quick, painless, humane way.

A guillotine had an approximately 4-meter (13-foot) frame with a heavy blade suspended from it. A two-part collar, called a lunette, held the victim's head in place, face down. The blade was slanted so that it chopped swiftly, rather than crushing the victim's neck. An executioner raised the blade by a rope and then let it drop. In less than half a second, the head rolled into a waiting basket, while a metal tray caught the blood.

The crowds that gathered to watch executions didn't like the guillotine at first—it was too quick and painless. With a guillotine, there wasn't enough of a show when a criminal was put to death. But eventually guillotining became popular. Vendors sold programs listing who was scheduled to die that day. Parents brought along their children to watch, and models of the guillotine were made as toys. The machine acquired nicknames such as Madame Guillotine, The Widow, and The Nation's Razor.

However, there were so many killings that eventually the crowds grew bored. Some experts suggest that as many as 15,000 people were guillotined during the French Revolution. Many more were shot or drowned, perhaps adding up to a total death toll as high as 40,000.

have no more tears to cry for you, my poor children; Goodbye! Goodbye!" A few hours later, her executioners came to hack off her hair—it mustn't get in the way of the guillotine's blade.

Marie Antoinette's humiliation and opposition were not over yet. While her husband had been driven to his execution in one of his own enclosed carriages, Marie Antoinette rode from the prison in a rough open cart. The gathered crowds gasped when they caught sight of her. Marie Antoinette was just 37 years old, but she looked decades older with her ragged hair and

"Courage! I have shown it for years; think you I shall lose it at the moment when my sufferings are to end?"

—MARIE ANTOINETTE, 1793

MASKED MURDER

France wasn't the only country in great turmoil in the late 1700s. Swedish royalty were also causing chaos in that country. King Gustav III was unpopular with both peasants and nobles. It wasn't long before his enemies began plotting to end his reign.

On March 16, 1792, Gustav attended a masked ball in Stockholm. Despite his disguise, the king was easy to identify because of the many military medals he insisted on wearing. A masked figure shot him, then the assassin's accomplices began to yell "Fire! Fire!" to cause confusion. Identifying the murderer was almost impossible because *everyone* was masked but assassin Jacob Johan Anckarström was arrested the next morning and soon confessed to the crime. Gustav died about two weeks later of gangrene, the decay and death of body tissue caused by a poor supply of blood.

worn clothes. Yet, despite being spat on and booed, the former queen sat tall in the wagon for the 45 long minutes it took to reach her final destination.

As the one-time royal stepped towards the guillotine, she accidentally stepped on the foot of her executioner. Marie Antoinette's last words were, "Monsieur, I beg your pardon. I did not do it on purpose." The crowds cheered loudly when the blade of the guillotine thudded down. Marie Antoinette's body was thrown on the grass, then dumped into an unmarked grave.

The French Revolution continued for another six years. Many thousands more people were killed, but none as famous as the king and queen. Louis probably wouldn't be much remembered today if he hadn't been his country's last king, but Marie Antoinette was one of France's most dazzling queens—and its most tragic.

The young queen became a symbol of the dangers of royal excess and its deadly end. She couldn't see how quickly life was changing around her and was too inexperienced to realize she must change her behavior before it was too late. Marie Antoinette had the misfortune to be born in such chaotic times, and she was overtaken by events she couldn't stop. Although she and Louis eventually found dignity and courage, it was too little, and far too late.

Empress Elisabeth

Beautiful Victim of Fate

Duchess

Ludovika of Bavaria was beside herself with worry. For years she'd been looking for a suitable husband for her daughter Elisabeth. Born in 1837, Princess Elisabeth was already 15, and although she was pretty, she was too shy and slim to catch any man's attention. Elisabeth, or Sisi, as she was nicknamed by her family, was also too willful and full of energy to sit still and learn her lessons. The princess should have learned all about court life, ceremony, and protocol. But instead Elisabeth preferred to ride horseback, swim, and climb mountains. Even her manners were poor. Who would ever marry such a girl, wondered her mother. What would become of her?

With a smile, Duchess Ludovika turned her thoughts to her daughter Hélène. Although Hélène was 18, Ludovika would have no trouble marrying her off. Princess Hélène was more beautiful than Elisabeth, better educated—and better mannered. Besides, Ludovika and her sister Archduchess Sophie had decided that Hélène would marry Sophie's son, Austria's Emperor Franz Josef.

What a catch! Franz Josef was one of the most powerful men in the world. Austria was Europe's second-largest state (only Russia was larger) and one of the richest. Franz Josef was also king of Hungary and head of many other territories. No wonder Ludovika was so delighted to think of him as Hélène's future husband.

The two mothers arranged that in August 1853, Duchess Ludovika would take Hélène from their home in Bavaria (now part of Germany) to a royal summer resort in Austria to meet Franz Josef. Ludovika and Sophie both expected the royal engagement would be announced shortly after. It was a good thing Ludovika had such a pleasant event to anticipate, because Elisabeth had fallen in love with a very unsuitable man, and the man's recent death had left her heartbroken.

Ludovika brought Elisabeth to the resort as well, thinking the trip might lift her spirits. And, thought the clever mother,

A trilogy of movies were made about the beautiful, doomed Elisabeth, and they're shown every Christmas on Austrian and German television. You can also watch the Sissi (as the empress was called in films and novels) movies on DVD.

SAVED BY A UNIFORM

In 1853, just a few months before he met Elisabeth, a would-be assassin stabbed the emperor in the neck. Luckily, Franz Josef was wearing a uniform, as he did frequently, and the stiff fabric of the collar saved his life. Although Franz Joseph was left badly injured and bleeding by the attack, he said coolly, "Now I am wounded along with my soldiers. I like that."

Elisabeth's friendship with Franz Josef's younger brother, Archduke Karl Ludwig, might develop into a romance. Ludovika could end up with two daughters married and off her hands.

But the two doting mothers hadn't allowed for the unexpected—which would have a hand in Elisabeth's marriage *and* her death.

When the sisters met Franz Josef, they were both dressed in black to mourn the recent death of an aunt. The color made Hélène look washed out, but it flattered Elisabeth. For Franz Josef, it was love at first sight—but not with the sister who'd been chosen for him by his mother and aunt. Elisabeth's sad, light brown eyes captivated Franz Josef. The young women he knew back home in Vienna were lively and bright—perhaps Elisabeth's melancholy gave her a unique charm in the emperor's eyes.

Franz Josef's younger brother immediately noticed his brother's interest. "At the moment when the Emperor caught sight of [Elisabeth]," Archduke Karl Ludwig reported, "an expression of such great pleasure appeared on his face that there was no longer any doubt whom he would choose."

The emperor's mother didn't give up without a fight. "Don't you think that Hélène is clever, that she has a beautiful, slender figure?" "Well, yes, a little grave and quiet, certainly pleasant and nice, yes," admitted her son, "but [Elisabeth]—such loveliness, such exuberance, like a little girl's and yet so sweet."

At first, the mothers were shocked by this change in their plans, and the two young sisters were confused. But the emperor was ecstatic and determined, and soon Elisabeth was delighted with her handsome, chivalrous beloved. Within days, Franz Josef and Elisabeth were engaged. The young duchess was happy but also worried about the traditions and rigidity of the life she was preparing to enter. "I love the Emperor so much," she sobbed to her mother. "If only he were not the Emperor!"

No wonder Elisabeth wished Franz Josef was anything but an emperor. Everyone now wanted to catch a glimpse of the young girl who had captured the heart of such an eligible bachelor. "I am on show like a freak in a circus," moaned Elisabeth. As well, the many aristocratic strangers Elisabeth was meeting intimidated her. The formalities of Austria's court seemed artificial to her and made aristocrats unapproachable by ordinary people. This was not the way she'd been raised, and she found her new life very difficult.

Elisabeth lacked aristocratic pride, which was viewed negatively by those in Vienna. She was used to shaking hands with anyone she met, but now she could merely allow her hand to be kissed, and only by specially privileged members of the upper class. The Austrian nobility looked down on her with scorn because she didn't fit in. And Elisabeth could see that she would have problems with her mother-in-law. Archduchess Sophie never really accepted her.

Despite these difficulties, the couple's wedding the following year was one of the most spectacular events ever in the history of Vienna. The richest people in Europe attended, sparkling in their most costly jewels and gems. About 15,000 candles lighted the church where Elisabeth and Franz Josef were married, and more than 70 bishops helped perform the marriage ceremony.

After the wedding, Elisabeth had to sit for almost two hours while princesses and duchesses filed past to kiss her hand. A gala banquet followed. Close on midnight, Elisabeth could finally go to her bedroom—accompanied by her mother and twelve servants carrying gold candelabras.

Despite the rich Austrians' concerns about their new empress, Elisabeth did one thing well. As a royal wife, she was expected to give birth to an heir to the throne. Elisabeth gave birth to a daughter, Sophie, in 1855, another daughter, Gisela, the year after that, and a son, Rudolf, in 1858. (Marie-Valerie was born later, in 1868.) Three babies in four years exhausted Elisabeth, but it didn't show—what people noticed was what a beautiful young woman she had become.

WHAT'S LOVE GOT TO DO WITH IT?

Elisabeth's mother, Ludovika, Elisabeth's aunt Sophie, and their seven sisters knew that as princesses, they were political pawns. They had no choice but to accept the men selected for them for marriage. Love didn't enter into it. In fact, the reading of love stories was forbidden at the Bavarian court so the young girls wouldn't grow up with any silly ideas about love and romance. When Ludovika married Max, Elisabeth's father, he told her that he didn't love her and was only marrying her because he was afraid of his powerful grandfather.

Elisabeth and Franz Josef were very much in love when they married. But it wouldn't have mattered how Elisabeth felt about the match. When asked if Elisabeth's feelings about the match were taken into account, Ludovika replied, "One does not send the Emperor of Austria packing."

Franz Joseph became engaged to Elisabeth in late August 1853."Every day I love Sisi more and more," Franz Joseph wrote, "and am more convinced that no one could be better suited to me."

Both commoners and aristocrats were enchanted by Elisabeth's looks. No longer a willful tomboy, she had a quiet, shy personality that charmed those she met and she had a graceful way of walking that made it seem as if she were floating. Austria became proud of the royal whose beauty was gossiped about all over the world.

Elisabeth began to work hard to maintain her looks. On a typical day, she rose early for a cold bath and a massage. Then she exercised—which very few people did at the time—and had a small breakfast. While her hair was being styled, Elisabeth wrote letters or read. By the time the empress was dressed, the morning was gone.

At lunch, Elisabeth took just a few minutes to eat some thin gravy. She hated having to sit down for a meal. After lunch, Elisabeth walked for hours, no matter what the weather. At the end of the afternoon, she changed her clothes and had her hair restyled. The only time Empress Elisabeth saw her husband was at dinner. Even then she ate little—at one point she gave up eating an evening meal and just drank a glass of beer or milk. No wonder she suffered from many health problems. After her meager dinner, Elisabeth left the table as quickly as possible to prepare for bed. Any official duty that disrupted this schedule she considered an annoyance.

Elisabeth and her family lived in the Hofburg Imperial Palace in Vienna, Austria. Today it's the official residence of Austria's president. There are also a number of museums in the palace, including the Sisi Museum, devoted to Empress Elisabeth.

As much as three hours of Elisabeth's day was needed for dressing, since sometimes she had to change several times for the many events that demanded her presence. It could take an hour just to lace her corset tight enough. To make sure her clothes fit perfectly, she was sewn into her dresses each time she wore them.

To stay thin, Elisabeth outfitted exercise rooms wherever she was living with bars, ropes, and rings. She exercised for hours, sometimes to the point of exhaustion. Once, she had some time to fill before meeting a group of archduchesses. So the empress worked out in her gym—despite the fact that she was already dressed in a long silk dress featuring a train edged with feathers. She swung about the room like a huge exotic bird.

The empress was obsessed with looking slender, so she didn't wear thick petticoats as other aristocratic women did.

OBSESSED WITH BEAUTY

Elisabeth's beauty made her a world-famous celebrity in the 1860s. She attracted huge crowds, and people jammed the streets to catch a glimpse of her. Foreign diplomats spread the word of her remarkable beauty. No matter where Elisabeth appeared, she stole the spotlight from all other women.

Not surprisingly, beauty became Elisabeth's obsession. She was especially occupied by her hair—it took an entire day to wash it. That's because Elisabeth's hair was very thick and so long that it flowed down to her feet. She tried many different mixtures for washing it—cognac and eggs was one of her favorites, using about 20 bottles of brandy.

Every day, it took Elisabeth and her hairdresser hours to care for her hair. The weight of her elaborate hairstyles sometimes gave Elisabeth headaches. On those days, her hair was held high with ribbons to take the weight off her head. When Elisabeth's tresses were brushed before bed, a white cloth was spread over the floor to catch any loose hairs, and the hairdresser also had to wear white. Every stray hair was collected when the brushing was over, and Elisabeth became upset if she thought there were too many.

Elisabeth's hair was strong and thick despite the unhealthy diets she followed. Most people had never heard of dieting at the time, and many royals ate large, rich meals and plenty of them. Elisabeth weighed herself twice a day, and if she had gained even a few ounces over her ideal weight of 50 kilograms (110 pounds)—far too little for her more than 172 centimeters (5 feet, 8 inches) in height—she immediately starved herself on a diet of just oranges and raw meat juice.

The empress's prime motive was always to hold on to the power she felt her beauty gave her. Perhaps her obsession also let her forget how obsessed the public was at catching even a glimpse of her and assessing her looks.

Instead, she wore long, thin underpants. What else did Elizabeth do in pursuit of beauty? She believed that sleeping with damp cloths on her hips kept her slim, as did drinking a mixture of egg whites with salt. Elisabeth also applied raw veal or mashed strawberries to her face each night. To keep her skin smooth and soft, she bathed in warm olive oil.

The empress discovered that her beauty gave her power and allowed her to get her own way, with her husband and others. For instance, she so disliked the haughty people who made up the court in Vienna that she tried to get away from the city as much as possible. That meant she went for long periods apart from her children and husband. Although Elisabeth was unhappy with her life at the court and with her marriage, the emperor was still madly in love with her and her beauty and found it hard to refuse Elisabeth's desire for escape or any of her other whims.

Elisabeth continued to be famous around the world for her extraordinary good looks. Sometimes this caused her great inconvenience, such as during the world exhibition held in Vienna in 1873. Nobles and well-off people traveled from all over to see amazing new technology, view works of art, and more. Actually, many of the dignitaries came to see Elisabeth. They wanted to decide for themselves about her legendary beauty.

Elisabeth soon tired of the ceremonies, dinners, and balls— and of being stared at. She left Vienna as soon as she could. That did not suit the Shah of Persia, who had come to Austria especially to see Elisabeth. He was so upset at missing a chance to look her over that he refused to leave. So Elisabeth angrily and reluctantly returned to Vienna to attend a party held in the shah's honor. Usually the Persian prince was very flirtatious with gorgeous women, but he became almost shy in the presence of her great beauty.

Shortly after the world exhibition ended, Elisabeth had a new obsession: horseback riding. She had an arena built at one of her homes and rode trick circus horses. When she heard about the

PUNCH'S FANCY PORTRAITS.—No. 22.

Punch, a British humor magazine, published this cartoon of Empress Elisabeth when she was spending so much time in England horseback riding.

hunting that was done on horseback in England, she was determined to try it. The English hunt involved riding large, strong horses very quickly over fields and high fences. It was especially difficult for women riding sidesaddle in their long skirts. But Elisabeth was determined to be the most beautiful and the best. She trained herself to be one of the top women riders in Europe. To hide herself from curious onlookers or passersby, she even managed to carry a fan as she rode.

Nine years later, Elisabeth had lost interest in horseback riding. She took up fencing but spent most of her time restlessly traveling between her homes in Austria and Hungary, as well as visiting other European countries. She fell into a deep depression when her beloved cousin, King Ludwig II of Bavaria, was declared insane and drowned shortly afterwards. And when Elisabeth's only son, Crown Prince Rudolf, died in 1889—people are still arguing if it was murder or suicide—the emperor feared she might never recover from her grief. She gave away much of her jewelry and wore almost nothing but black from then on.

The empress continued to leave Austria as often as she could, for as long as she could, but her journeys became more pointless. By train or yacht, she roamed France, Greece, Spain, and many other countries. As Elisabeth grew older, her skin became wrinkled and weather-beaten because of her starvation diets and the time she spent outdoors. When out walking with a lady-in-waiting, she always shielded her face from passersby with a fan or umbrella. Despite her aching joints, Elisabeth still spent hours every day exercising, lifting weights, and doing gymnastics. She refused to have her photograph taken, so photographers touched up earlier photos of her to make them look more current. Despite her conviction that her beauty was a thing of the past, men still were enamored with her.

In the late summer of 1898, Elisabeth's wanderings took her to the Swiss city of Geneva to see the town's beautiful mountains and lake. Since she was there for just one night, she refused to be protected by security guards, as the Swiss police recommended strongly to any high-born person.

Elisabeth did try to conceal her identity by traveling under the false name of Countess von Hohenembs. Although she used this name at her hotel, a local newspaper reported not only that Empress Elisabeth was in Geneva but also where she was staying.

Also in Geneva at that time was Luigi Lucheni. He dreamed of becoming famous by assassinating someone of royal birth. He'd come to the Swiss city because he'd heard a French duke planned to visit the city. Lucheni had prepared himself by buying a file, then honing the blade until it was razor sharp. He even consulted a medical book to learn the best place to stab a victim. "How I would like to kill someone," Lucheni wrote in his diary, "but it must be someone important so it gets in the papers."

When word came that the duke had changed his mind, Lucheni was furious. He didn't have the money to travel elsewhere to stalk

"I WOULD LIKE TO DIE ALONE, FAR FROM MY LOVED ONES, AND FOR DEATH TO TAKE ME UNAWARES."

—EMPRESS ELISABETH

SKINNY DAGGER

The knife that Luigi Lucheni used to stab Empress Elisabeth is known as a stiletto, a dagger with a long, narrow blade. It was a favorite weapon among assassins because it was easy to conceal up a sleeve or in a jacket. The stiletto first became popular in fights between heavily armored knights— the thin knife could easily slip between gaps in the knights' armor.

Elisabeth was so well loved by the general public that she traveled with few bodyguards. That's why Lucheni was able to get close to her so easily (far right).

another royal victim. What could he do now? Lucheni was determined to make a statement by killing a monarch and any one would do.

At that point, fate intervened. Lucheni happened to pick up a newspaper. Angry and frustrated, Lucheni skimmed the articles without interest until one grabbed his attention. With great excitement, he read that Empress Elisabeth was nearby. Lucheni had found a new target.

On the morning of September 10, Lucheni was waiting outside Elisabeth's hotel, his stiletto knife carefully concealed in his right sleeve. He'd discovered the empress would be leaving Geneva by ship, and he knew which one—he'd already seen her servant depart with the luggage.

Carrying her usual fan and parasol, Elisabeth left the hotel along with her lady-in-waiting, Irma. Unknown to them, Lucheni was intently watching their every move. Elisabeth had only a short distance to walk to the boat, but that was enough for her assassin. As the women passed him, Lucheni lunged. Taking a quick look under the umbrella to make sure he had the right victim, he stabbed at Elisabeth's heart.

Lucheni fled but was captured by witnesses and marched to the police station. Elizabeth had fallen heavily onto the ground, but got up quickly, seemingly unharmed. Her thick, pinned-up hair had protected her head when she fell, and Lucheni's dagger seemed to have missed its target. Still, a hotel worker who had witnessed the attack urged Elisabeth and Irma to return to the hotel to recover. But the empress refused. She was determined to continue her journey.

As the two women hurried toward the ship, they wondered what the attacker had wanted. The empress finally decided Lucheni had simply wanted to rob them. Putting the incident behind them, the women boarded the boat.

The ship had only just departed when Elisabeth suddenly collapsed. Irma thought she'd merely fainted from the shock of

UNHAPPY ANARCHIST

Growing up in foster homes and orphanages and poor all of his life, Luigi Lucheni had a grudge against people who were rich or royal. He said he had killed Elisabeth "… as part of the war on the rich and great. A Lucheni kills an empress but would never kill a washerwoman."

Lucheni loved the attention he received for killing the empress. He felt the assassination was the most important thing he had ever done. In his dreams, the assassination of a royal had always ended with Lucheni's glorious execution. He was extremely disappointed when he found out he wouldn't be executed—there was no death penalty in Switzerland, where the crime took place.

Meanwhile, Lucheni so enjoyed his new fame and the letters he received in jail that eventually prison officials refused to give him his mail. So he never saw a death threat signed by 16,000 women and girls from Vienna that included many bloodthirsty suggestions for his slow, painful death.

the recent attack. So the lady-in-waiting quickly unbuttoned her mistress's blouse and corset to rub her chest and improve the blood flow. Irma gasped in horror when she saw a tiny brownish stain and a hole in Elisabeth's camisole. Elisabeth had actually been stabbed in the heart by the attacker.

The captain turned the ship back to Geneva immediately, and Elisabeth was carried to the hotel as quickly as possible. But it was too late. Elisabeth died soon after she arrived. Her last words were, "What happened to me?" Doctors later deduced that Lucheni's file had been so narrow and sharp that Elisabeth's wound was very tiny. Her heart had stopped only gradually, which was why she had been able to walk to the ship.

Elisabeth's husband was heartbroken at the news. "You do not know how much I loved this woman," Franz Josef mourned to their daughter Marie-Valerie. The empress's murder amazed and terrified Europe's royalty—assassination was the end they all most feared. As well, since Elisabeth had long ago given up politics and public appearances, her murder seemed inexplicable.

When Lucheni killed Elisabeth, he murdered Europe's most beautiful and fascinating royal. The empress's relentless travels were over. One of the world's most famous royal beauties was finally at rest.

The Romanovs

Russia's Doomed Royals

At last, sighed Czarina Alexandra as she cuddled her newborn son, Alexei, a boy to inherit the throne of Russia. Now everything will be better for our country. Everything will be all right.

Alexandra couldn't have been more wrong.

Czar Nikolay Romanov, the baby's father, was emperor of Russia. At the beginning of the 1900s, his country was the largest empire on Earth, covering more than one-sixth of the entire world. Nikolay and his wife, Alexandra, and their five children enjoyed a life of unimaginable wealth and incredible power.

For most of the year, the Romanov family lived at Tsarskoye Selo ("Tsar's village") in the country outside of St. Petersburg (then Russia's capital). High iron railings surrounded the 325 hectares (800 acres) of gardens, fountains, and even an artificial lake. The family lived in Alexander Palace, the smaller of the two palaces on the grounds: it had *only* 100 rooms. The nearby Catherine Palace dwarfed the family's home and was used only for formal occasions.

CORONATION CATASTROPHE

When Nikolay was crowned czar in May 1896, more than 1 million Russians crowded into Moscow. It was tradition that at the coronation the czar provided unlimited food for his subjects, as well as souvenirs. So many people in the country were starving that they showed up just to get something to eat. The size of the crowd created a stampede, and more than 1,200 peasants were trampled and killed.

Still, the coronation party was not canceled, despite the tragedy, and that's what people remembered: that their new Czar and Czarina danced while Russians died, even though Nikolay and Alexandra donated generously to the families of the dead. But it's no wonder the new emperor quickly gained the nickname Bloody Nikolay.

The Catherine Palace was known for being incredibly lavish and luxurious. Real gold was used to decorate it, both inside and out.

During the winter, the family moved to the stunning Winter Palace in St. Petersburg. This home covered three city blocks and was furnished inside with rich marble, glittering chandeliers, and huge mirrors. Nikolay and Alexandra joined the rest of Russia's upper class attending lavish balls, ballets, concerts, and operas, where all the women wore expensive dresses and priceless jewels.

Nikolay wasn't very interested in being emperor. He was charming but very shy and not especially smart. He found it hard to make decisions and so usually weakly did what his wife told him to do. Nikolay's father had died unexpectedly of kidney disease, before Nikolay had been trained to take over from him. The son tried to use the same harsh, controlling style his father had, but that approach was now outdated. Times were changing, and royalty was losing its power in Russia as the country edged toward revolution.

Nikolay's family concerned him more than his country. Although the czar and czarina loved their four daughters— Olga, Tatiana, Maria, and Anastasia—they desperately wished for a son to inherit the Russian throne. So they were delighted in August 1904 when Alexandra gave birth to Alexei. But their delight turned to despair when Alexei was just six weeks old and Alexandra noticed he was bleeding from his navel.

The czarina gasped in horror. She knew this was a symptom of hemophilia, the disease that had killed her brother and her uncle. It prevents a person's blood from clotting normally. Even a slight bruise can cause painful and deadly internal bleeding. Alexei's parents worried that Russians would never accept their son as their future ruler if they knew he was unhealthy, so they hid his true condition from the country and the world. The czar and his family spent longer periods of time away from the public in order to protect Alexei.

Before Alexandra married Nikolay in 1894, she was called Princess Alix. She was a much-loved granddaughter of England's Queen Victoria.

Nikolay, known as "Nicky" to his close family and friends, fell in love with Alexandra when he was sixteen and she was just twelve.

LIKE GRANDFATHER, LIKE GRANDSON

Nikolay's grandfather, Czar Alexander, brought changes to Russia, such as increasing the rights of the poor and altering the government and justice system. Not everyone agreed with his changes and that resulted in many assassination attempts against him. In 1881, Alexander survived the bombing of his carriage, but he was killed when a second bomb exploded at his feet.

An assassin also tried to kill Nikolay. Before he became czar, Nikolay traveled a lot, including visiting Japan in 1891. While there, he was attacked by a man waving a sword. Luckily, Nikolay's cousin used his cane to fend off the man. The future czar was left with a scar on his forehead for the rest of his life—as well as a bitter hatred for Japan.

Meanwhile, workers and peasants who lived in extreme poverty, some in wretched slums, were starving. The common people grew increasingly angry at the laws Nikolay imposed, which kept them in an impoverished condition.

More troubles were ahead for Nikolay. In 1904 and 1905, the Russian army lost more than 40,000 soldiers in a war against Japan. Many Russians questioned Nikolay's ability to rule.

In 1905, the countrywide unhappiness erupted into violent strikes and a noisy uprising. On Sunday, January 22, more than 50,000 workers from St. Petersburg's factories began marching to the Winter Palace to demand help. There was just one problem—the marchers and organizers hadn't bothered to make sure Nikolay was at the Winter Palace. In fact, he was in Tsarskoye Selo and didn't find out about the protest until it was too late.

The protesters were peaceful and unarmed, but a government official ordered armed troops into the city. As the marchers drew closer to the Winter Palace, they ignored official orders to end their protest. They pressed forward, convinced their czar would never allow the soldiers to shoot at his subjects. Of course, the czar knew nothing of what was going on. The troops opened fire on the protesters, killing 200 people, including children, and wounding 800. People blamed the czar for the tragedy that became known as Bloody Sunday.

Meanwhile, Alexandra was desperately searching for a way to help her son. She heard of a holy man who was supposed to have miraculous powers to heal the sick through prayer, as well as to foretell the future. Sure enough, Grigori Rasputin seemed able to help Alexei every time the boy's bleeding started.

To this day, no one knows how Rasputin cured Alexei. Some historians think he used hypnosis; others say he simply encouraged Alexei to rest so that the boy's body could heal itself. Although Rasputin could be rude and smell of liquor, the czar and czarina believed he was a man of God. He became a close friend of the royal family.

Rasputin was an intense, rough-looking man. Czar Nikolay called him a "holy man" and "our friend," which shows how important Rasputin was to the royal family.

Rasputin was not popular beyond the palace, however. As the public clamored for changes, Rasputin advised Alexandra against them. Nikolay did agree to a form of elected government, but he tried to retain as much royal power as he could. Revolution and the disintegration of Nikolay's empire were from then on inevitable.

The Romanov children remained unaware of these growing problems. They spent their summers cruising on a magnificent yacht or playing at the beach. In winter they skated, or tobogganed down an artificial hill. The girls had custom-made dolls and dollhouses, and Alexei dressed up in child-sized army officer uniforms.

The two older daughters, Olga and Tatiana, were known

"Tsar of the land of Russia ... if it was your relations who have wrought my death, then no one in the family ... will remain alive for more than two years. They will be killed by the Russian people."

—RASPUTIN, 1916
(PART OF A LETTER TO ALEXANDRA WRITTEN JUST WEEKS BEFORE RASPUTIN WAS ASSASSINATED)

Nickolay and Alexandra's children were (left to right) Maria, Tatiana, Anastasia, Olga, and Alexei.

as "the big pair" within the family; Maria and Anastasia were "the little pair." Because their mother kept the four girls separate from the rest of the world, they became very close. They often dressed alike and went by the group name OTMA, formed from the first letter of each of their names. All of the girls were very protective of their brother. They took turns spending time with Alexei to make sure he didn't accidentally bruise himself.

Before long, both royals and peasants would be caught up in the changes sweeping the country. When Austria's Archduke Franz Ferdinand was murdered by a Serbian assassin in 1914, Austria complained to Serbia, and Russia took Serbia's side. Austria and Russia began threatening each other and before long, Europe was embroiled in the First World War.

At first, protesting workers and angry revolutionaries enthusiastically joined to fight for the glory of their country. Soldiers marched off to war full of nationalistic pride. In the first year of the war, Russian troops fought bravely and won important victories against Austria and Germany.

Unfortunately for the royal family, it seemed that no matter what they did, the Russian public found fault with it. Although the czarina opened a ward for wounded officers at the Winter Palace, nursed soldiers with great dedication, and recruited her older daughters to help, many people felt she wasn't doing enough. As well, Alexandra had been born in Germany—now Russia's enemy—and Russians could not forget this. They still didn't trust her loyalty to Russia.

Nikolay was convinced by Rasputin that the czar should be leading the Russian army, so he headed to the battlefield. Although he meant well, he was unprepared and characteristically indecisive. Because of his poor leadership, the losses of Russian troops in the First World War were staggering: by the end of October 1916, more than 1.5 million soldiers had died, 2 million were prisoners of war, and 1 million were missing. The men began to mutiny and desert. They were hungry and had no shoes, ammunition, or, often, weapons.

While Nikolay was leading the army, Alexandra was left in control of the country. She wrote to Nikolay constantly to discuss any decisions she made, but she relied more and more on Rasputin for advice. Some Russians felt that he was ruling their country. They resented that a peasant, whom many considered a fraud, held so much power. While people continued to lose confidence in Nikolay, neither he nor Alexandra did anything to calm the unrest.

In December 1916, a group decided something had to be done about the bizarre priest and his power over the royal family. Rasputin had to die. The would-be assassins included the czar's cousin and the husband of the czar's niece. The men invited Rasputin to dine and they fed him poisoned cakes and wine. Amazingly, the toxic food and drink seemed to have no effect. Next the killers tried shooting Rasputin. The men were just congratulating themselves that the so-called holy man was dead—when miraculously he suddenly sprang up at them!

EARTH-SHATTERING ASSASSINATION

In the early 1900s, many European countries seemed to be itching for an excuse to go to war. An unimportant visit by an almost unknown royal eventually gave it to them.

In 1914, Austrian Archduke Franz Ferdinand was scheduled to visit Sarajevo in Bosnia-Herzegovina. A group of Serbian assassins was waiting for him. As Franz Ferdinand drove into Sarajevo on June 28, 1914, a grenade just missed his car but hurt people in the surrounding crowd. The archduke insisted on driving to the hospital to visit the wounded. That gave the assassins another chance—and this time there was no mistake. Franz Ferdinand was shot by Serbian Gavrilo Princip, and less than two months later Austria declared war on Serbia. The First World War had begun.

PISTOL POWER

Pistols were frequently used by Nikolay's guards and by his opponents. These small handguns had become favorite weapons of assassins soon after they were invented in the 1500s. Some people say the pistol gets its name from the city where it was first made: Pistoia, Italy.

Over the course of the evening, the assassins shot Rasputin again and again, and beat him too, but he refused to die. Finally they dumped him in an icy river. The next day, Rasputin was pulled frozen from the water. The so-called Mad Monk was finally dead. Czarina Alexandra was inconsolable. Because of unrest in the country and hostility toward Rasputin and the royal family, the government advised the family to bury the monk quietly, with little ceremony.

In early 1917, riots broke out in St. Petersburg. People were starving and were growing increasingly resentful of the war. Nikolay commanded his troops to restore order, but the soldiers refused to fire on the mob. In fact, many of them joined the workers, who were calling for the creation of a society fair to all. It became known as the February Revolution.

By March 15, the Russian government felt there was only one way to save the country: the czar must abdicate his throne. Nikolay sadly agreed, though he had no idea of how lawlessness and violence had spread throughout the country. One observer wrote: "… [he] transformed himself from the ruler of all Russia to a person with no rights whatsoever, at the mercy of heaven only knows what questionable characters." Nikolay made his younger brother Grand Duke Mikhail czar in his place, but he gave up the crown a day later. More than three hundred years of royal rule in Russia was now over. "All around me," wrote Nikolay in his diary, "I see treachery, cowardice and deceit." Unfortunately, he'd been too inexperienced to see it earlier and overcome it.

No longer a czar, Nikolay returned to his family at Alexander Palace, where they were held prisoner. The children continued with their lessons, as well as embroidery and drawing. One thing was very different—the royal family had grown up with court etiquette that dictated no one could talk to the Romanovs unless invited to speak. Now the soldiers guarding them interrupted them rudely, taunted them, and seemed to delight in finding new ways to humiliate the family. The Romanovs were allowed to take walks outside the palace only when their guards allowed it. Crowds gathered at the gates to hurl insults at them.

The Russian Revolution continued. Revolutionaries known as Bolsheviks began to gain popularity. This party believed in socialism, a system for producing and distributing food and other goods that are owned by everyone in the community or by a central government. It was the complete opposite of being ruled by a czar who had all of the power and privilege while the poor had almost nothing. No wonder it sounded enticing to the starving people of Russia. Needless to say, the Bolsheviks were opposed to the idea of royalty.

The Romanovs' enemies used a hammer and sickle as a symbol. The hammer represents industrial workers and the sickle (a tool for cutting grass and grain) symbolizes farm workers. Later the hammer and sickle became a symbol of the Soviet Union.

Chaos and fighting between the various groups increased in St. Petersburg. Government officials feared that the Romanovs were no longer safe living close to the capital with its many Bolsheviks. So in August 1917 the royal family was sent to Tobolsk, Siberia, far from the uproar of the revolution. Life there was tolerable, although their house was very cold in winter, and the food was plain. The children complained of boredom.

In October, the Bolsheviks seized power in what became known as the October Revolution, or Red October. Life was no better for the poor Russian workers—the Bolshevik leaders were brutal and cruelly eliminated anyone who stood in their way. Because the town of Tobolsk could only be reached by horse and cart, it took several weeks for the news of the revolution to reach the former royals. Nikolay was devastated. With the Bolsheviks in power, the family finally realized the danger that surrounded them. They found what happiness they could in being together, reading, and doing what they could to keep busy. They tried not to think about the horrors that might be ahead.

In April 1918, the Bolsheviks ordered Nikolay to leave Tobolsk. Alexandra decided she must stay by his side and would also bring their daughter Maria. The other three girls stayed behind to care for their brother—who was too sick to be moved.

"WHAT SHALL THE FUTURE BRING TO MY POOR CHILDREN? MY HEART BREAKS THINKING OF THEM."

—CZARINA ALEXANDRA, 1917

Nikolay, Alexandra, and Maria had no idea where they were going. The children left behind were scared but clung to the hope that they would soon see their parents again. "Father asks to … remember that the evil which is now in the world will become yet more powerful," said Olga, "and that it is not evil which conquers evil, but only love …"

Days later, Alexandra wrote to her children from a house in Ekaterinburg, more than 485 kilometers (300 miles) away. The Bolsheviks were already sinisterly calling this building the "House of Special Purpose." In her letter, Alexandra instructed her daughters to "dispose of the medicines as had been agreed." The girls knew this was code for them to hide the family's jewels. If the Romanovs managed to escape from Russia, they could sell the jewelry to survive. Immediately Anastasia, Olga, and Tatiana began sewing jewels into the hems of their skirts, concealing them in ornate buttons, and tucking them into hats and corsets.

In May, the three girls and their brother were united with their parents in Ekaterinburg. The windows of their latest prison were nailed shut and whitewashed so the Romanovs could see nothing outside. Food was scarce, and the Bolshevik revolutionaries guarding them were insulting and abusive. The only desperate hope Nikolay and Alexandra held on to was that forces loyal to them were fighting their enemies somewhere nearby. If the Romanovs' allies could seize control of Ekaterinburg from the Bolsheviks, the family would be saved. The royals anxiously prayed for an early rescue.

Just after midnight on July 17, 1918, Nikolay and his family were awakened and ordered to dress. The fighting was getting closer, they were told, and for their own safety they were to move to the basement of the house. In truth, the Bolsheviks were afraid that if the royal family's protectors were able to rescue them, the family could inspire their remaining forces. There was only one way to prevent that.

The family's doctor and three of their servants joined the unsuspecting family in a small room in the basement. Suddenly armed soldiers appeared at the doorway. The royal family was shocked. "Your relatives have tried to save you," the commander of the soldiers informed them. "They have failed, and we are obliged to shoot you all."

"What?" cried the czar. The commander repeated the order as the Romanovs began wailing in terror.

Almost immediately, the soldiers began shooting. They wanted to be able to later brag of being the one who shot the czar, so their guns were aimed on him. In the crowd of victims, the czar died first, followed closely by his wife. But when the soldiers shot at the daughters, the bullets bounced off the girls and ricocheted wildly around the room. Were these royal daughters bulletproof?

It was payday for the soldiers, and most of them were drunk. The apparent miracle nearly made the soldiers run in fear. In the midst of the clouds of gunsmoke and stench of gunpowder, the soldiers began stabbing and clubbing their victims, anything to finally silence them. Blood ran in streams from the Romanovs' bodies as the soldiers bayoneted and kicked them to death. The bullets, which should have finished the girls, had been deflected by the stash of jewels the princesses had sewn into their corsets.

The slaughter lasted nearly 30 minutes. Stories were later told of how some of the children were still alive and sat up or cried out as the bodies were carried out of the "House of Special Purpose" and dumped in a waiting truck, which raced off into the night. For now, the deaths must be kept secret. The dead family and attendants had to be out of Ekaterinburg before dawn.

No one knows for sure what happened next, but it's likely the truck driver dropped the corpses into a nearby mine. Too many people managed to find the burial spot,

IMPRISONMENT

The Bolsheviks made sure the Romanovs' imprisonment at Ekaterinburg was as miserable and humiliating as possible. Doors were removed from most of the rooms, so there was little privacy. Even the bathroom doors were taken down, and the family members were never allowed to go to the washroom alone. The bathroom walls were covered with filthy jokes, excrement, and insults. The guards sometimes spat in the Romanovs' food or didn't feed them at all. The meal usually consisted of bread and tea, or whatever was left over from the guards' dinner.

The Bolsheviks delighted in scaring the family. One of the daughters was shot at when she tried to open a window. When Anastasia asked to retrieve a pair of shoes from her luggage, she was told she didn't need them—the ones she was wearing would last as long as she would.

When the Romanovs and their servants had gathered in the basement, they were told a photograph would be taken to prove to the Russian people that they were still alive. So the royal family was arranged into two rows. Then the soldiers burst in and opened fire.

though, so the dead were buried in a shallow grave close by. The grave was doused with sulfuric acid to reduce the smell and to make the bodies decay rapidly. Some of the gravediggers later said that two of the deceased had been burned. That was done so that if the remaining bodies were ever found, it would be difficult to count them. What they didn't realize was that the corpses had been so badly disfigured in the shooting that they were already almost impossible to recognize. No one knew for sure who they were burning.

The Bolsheviks tried to confuse the Russian people by leaking misinformation about the killings. At first they reported that only Nikolay had been executed. People believed the rest of the family had escaped, and miraculous sightings of the "remaining" Romanovs began to occur. The mystery over the family's fate only deepened over the years.

The Romanovs' bones lay in their shallow grave for almost 60 years, until 1976, when amateur researchers in Russia pieced together information from special archives and identified the burial site. The researchers were frightened by the political situation in Russia at the time, so they kept their findings unreported until 1989.

When the grave was finally reopened in 1991, the researchers discovered two bodies were missing. One of them was certainly Alexei's, but no one could agree on which young girl was missing. Some said Anastasia, others said Maria. It was impossible to know for sure.

Experts compared the DNA in the bones to the DNA of living relatives of the Romanovs for positive identification. Prince Philip, husband of England's Queen Elizabeth, is a grandson of Alexandra's sister Victoria. Philip allowed his blood to be tested, and a match to Alexandra was confirmed. Bones thought to be the czar's were tested in a similar way and identified.

The family's bones sat in Russian laboratories for years—no one could decide where the Romanovs should be reburied.

ANASTASIA

So many wild rumors circulated after the Romanovs were murdered that many people believed not all the family members actually had been killed. The Romanov most often whispered to still be alive was the czar's young daughter Anastasia.

On February 17, 1920, a young woman was rescued from a canal in Berlin, Germany, where she'd tried to commit suicide. For a long time she would not give her name; in fact, she hardly spoke at all. "If people knew who I am, I would not be here," was one of the few things she said. Authorities were puzzled when they noticed that the woman showed marks of having been stabbed a number of times.

Anna Anderson, as she came to be known, spent two years in a mental asylum. When she finally began to talk, she saw a photograph of Anastasia and pointed out how much they looked alike. Other people noticed this too, and relatives of the Romanovs came to meet her. Some were convinced by Anna's appearance and her knowledge of the royal family that she was Anastasia; others were certain she was an imposter. Oddly, she would speak Russian only in her sleep or when she thought she wasn't being "tested." When asked why, Anna answered, "Because it was the last language we heard in that house."

When Anna died in 1984, the mystery of her true identity had still not been solved. Was she or wasn't she the lost Romanov? DNA evidence a decade later indicated she couldn't be Anastasia. At almost the same time, face and ear comparisons, evidence used in court to legally identify people, were done between photos of Anna and Anastasia. These showed that Anna *was* Anastasia. The truth about Anna Anderson's real identify died with her, but the mystery still fascinates people.

Some questioned why these victims should be treated any differently from other victims of the Revolution, while others wondered whether they should be laid to rest in Ekaterinburg, where they were murdered and where a huge church now stands. Or should the family be entombed in St. Petersburg, beside their ancestors?

The sides argued back and forth. Finally in 1998, 80 years after the Romanovs were executed, their bones were buried with honor in a cathedral in St. Petersburg. The conflicting stories about their deaths continued. A poll of Russians conducted that same year showed that only 47 percent believed the remains actually belong to the royal family.

The mystery of the Romanovs' death was in the news again in 2007 when the bones of two young people were found near the site of the royal family's original grave. Experts argued whether or not these were the remains of Alexei and one of his sisters.

Nikolay was the last czar of Russia. The tidal wave of the Russian Revolution brought a shattering end to the monarchy and the glittering world of the Romanovs. Perhaps a stronger, better-trained, and more progressive czar could have slowed the pace of change in the country; however, this charming but weak man and his family were doomed before he took Russia's throne. The legends surrounding the murder of Russia's last royals still haunt the country and the whole world.

Modern Murders

Most royals around the world today have little power. Instead, in many countries prime ministers and presidents are elected to make decisions on behalf of their citizens. If these officials make too many unpopular choices, they usually get voted out—not murdered.

Some royal murders, or attempted murders, still take place. Most receive little publicity, however, for a few reasons. For instance, sometimes the would-be murderer is seeking fame, so police try their best to make sure the killer doesn't achieve that goal. As well, police don't want to encourage copycat murders.

Did you know that England's current royal family has been attacked many times? While riding in parades, attending ceremonies, or even while relaxing at Buckingham Palace, Queen Elizabeth still has to face the possibility that someone will try to kill her. In June 1981, blank shots were fired at her while she was on horseback in a ceremony. About a year later, an intruder broke into the sleeping queen's bedroom. She coolly chatted with him until the police arrived.

Queen Elizabeth and others in the British royal family continue to walk among crowds despite the danger. Many of the people around them are actually plainclothes police, carefully watching for assassins.

But not all modern murderers of monarchs can be stopped. Here are some royal murders from the last 80 years.

Superstitious Royal

Many people are afraid of Friday the 13th. But King Alexander I of Yugoslavia believed Tuesday—every Tuesday—was an unlucky day for him. No wonder: three of his relatives had died on that day. So the king made sure he never took part in any public ceremonies or events on that weekday.

However, on Tuesday, October 9, 1934, Alexander had no choice. Government officials had arranged for him to drive

Before he became king, Alexander was a very successful army commander.

through the streets of Marseilles, France, in a slow-moving, open car during a visit to improve his country's ties with the French. Like it or not, Alexander had to take part in the tour.

Assassin Vlado Chernozemski was waiting. A cold-blooded killer, he once said, "Killing a man is nothing more to me than uprooting a tree." Chernozemski was working for an Italian group that wanted to take over part of Yugoslavia. As Alexander's car drove by, the killer leapt onto the side of it and shot the king twice. The monarch died within minutes.

At this point, Chernozemski's accomplice was supposed to start throwing bombs at the crowd to cause confusion so the assassin could escape. But this Tuesday was unlucky for Chernozemski too. He soon discovered the other man had fled in fear. It was up to

Chernozemski to create a diversion, so he fired into the throng, killing two bystanders. A guard slashed at Chernozemski with a saber, then a police officer shot him dead. The mob took its revenge by kicking and tearing at the assassin's body.

Alexander's murder became famous around the world not because he was an especially important king, but because his killing was one of the first assassinations ever captured on film. The king happened to die right in front of a nearby camera operator, who was able to film the royal death.

Mysterious End

To this day, no one really knows what killed Boris III, Czar of Bulgaria—or where he's buried. When the Second World War began in 1939, his country was neutral; it did not help the Nazis in Germany or assist Canada, Britain, and the other Allies. But by 1941, Boris had reluctantly sided with the Germans, as his country had done in the First World War.

Soon Adolf Hitler, the German leader, was furious that Bulgaria wasn't helping his side enough. So in August 1943, Hitler summoned Boris to a meeting in Berlin, Germany. At the meeting Hitler became incensed when Boris refused to involve Bulgaria further in the war.

Shaken by Hitler's wrath, Boris flew home. Then, just a few days later, Bulgaria's king unexpectedly died. The official cause of death was heart failure, but it seemed strange that Boris died so soon after the angry meeting with the German leader. Stories sprang up that he'd been poisoned by Hitler or that Hitler had arranged to reduce the oxygen on his airplane home. No one ever knew for sure why or how Boris died.

More mystery was soon to follow. After a large, impressive funeral, Boris's coffin was whisked away and buried in Bulgaria's largest and most important monastery. Then the next year the

Boris became king in 1918. Seven years later, there were two assassination attempts against him, but Boris survived them both.

coffin was dug up and secretly buried in the yard at the Bulgarian royal palace.

Later the coffin was moved again, and no one knows where it ended up. When the royal palace yard was excavated, all that was found of Boris was his heart, in a glass cylinder. It was reburied back at the monastery, but the location of the rest of Boris's body is still a mystery.

Middle Eastern Murder

King Abdullah Ibn Hussein of Jordan was killed because of his secret negotiations with another country. The king wanted to hold on to the West Bank of the Jordan River, which his country had won in battle. Most Arabs thought this land would become home to Palestinians, not be a part of Jordan. Despite Abdullah's plans, he soon realized that he couldn't keep the land by force. Although he'd fought against Israel in the past, he began secret negotiations with the Israelis over the territory.

Radical Palestinians found out about the king's undercover talks with Israel and wanted them stopped. On July 20, 1951, Abdullah entered a mosque in the Old City of Jerusalem. When a sheik stepped forward to pay his respects to the monarch, the king's guards moved back to allow the sheik to pass. Just then, a tailor's apprentice pushed past him. The apprentice, Mustafa Ashu, fired just a single shot at Abdullah, but it was murderously accurate. The king was dead before he even hit the floor.

Suddenly the mosque was full of flying bullets. The king's bodyguards instantly opened fire to kill Ashu. They succeeded but shot so recklessly that they also killed more than 20 people in the mosque and wounded about 100 others. Eventually all of Ashu's conspirators were rounded up and executed. Although they all died, they achieved their goal: negotiations between Jordan and Israel died along with King Abdullah. The Middle East continues to be one of the most troubled areas in the world.

When King Abdullah was shot, his grandson was also hit. But a medal that King Abdullah had insisted the younger man wear on his chest deflected the bullet and saved his life.

Brotherly Love?

King Faisal was known as a reformer and modernizer.

On March 25, 1975, King Faisal of Saudi Arabia was holding a royal audience at his palace in Riyadh. This weekly event, called a *majlis,* was a chance for people to bring the king requests or petitions. On this day many people were waiting to speak to him, including the king's nephew, Prince Faisal Ibu Musaid.

As the prince approached his uncle, the older man bent forward so his nephew could kiss him on the nose, which is a sign of respect. Instead of kissing him, Prince Musaid suddenly pulled out a gun and calmly fired three bullets right at King Faisal's face. Despite a doctor's desperate efforts, the king was soon dead.

No one knows for sure why the prince assassinated his uncle. Some people suggest he was avenging the death of his older brother, Khaled, who died 10 years earlier. This prince was very conservative and objected to the introduction of television to Saudi Arabia because he felt it was anti-Islamic. He joined a group trying to tear down a television tower. Khaled and the others fired on the tower's guards, who fired back, killing Khaled.

When King Faisal was asked to punish the guard for shooting Khaled, the king refused, saying that his nephew had been breaking the law. How could King Faisal know that a decade later he would pay for his decision with his own life?

Whatever the reason for his actions, Prince Musaid was diagnosed as mentally unbalanced. Although King Faisal's last words were to beg that his assassin not be executed, Musaid was not spared. He was punished in the traditional way under Islamic law: beheading in a public square.

symbolic Assassination

Sometimes simply having a royal connection can be dangerous. Louis Mountbatten, 1st Earl Mountbatten of Burma, found that out in 1979.

As a young man, Mountbatten had visited Russia's doomed royal family. There, he fell in love with Nikolay and Alexandra's daughter Maria and always kept her photo by his bedside.

Mountbatten was a great-grandson of England's Queen Victoria. As a boy he was very friendly with the Romanov children of the doomed royal family of Russia (see the previous chapter). Mountbatten was also a distant cousin of Queen Elizabeth II; an uncle of her husband, Prince Philip; and honorary godfather to Elizabeth and Philip's son, Prince Charles. While Mountbatten had many titles, he had no real power.

The Irish Republican Army (IRA) knew this, but to them Mountbatten still represented the British royal family. And England's royals were a symbol of what the IRA members saw as the English occupation of their country, an occupation they had vowed to end. The IRA also was aware that Lord Mountbatten was much less well guarded than was Queen Elizabeth's immediate family.

It was well known that Mountbatten usually spent a few weeks every summer at a castle on the Irish coast. The IRA was often in the area, the local police knew. They warned Mountbatten to be careful, and they kept a close watch on the castle. But in August 1979, no one was guarding Mountbatten's boat, moored at a public dock. It was easy for the IRA to stealthily place a radio-controlled bomb on the boat, then wait for Mountbatten to board.

On August 27, Mountbatten, with some friends and family, headed out for a day on the boat. They were just offshore when the bomb was detonated, exploding the boat into thousands of pieces. All the passengers were thrown from the boat, and Lord Mountbatten and three others died. The assassin was quickly caught, but the IRA received a lot of news coverage for their deadly deed.

just Like Romeo and juliet

In the tale of Romeo and Juliet, the young lovers are desperate because, thanks to their feuding families, they can't be together. Despite the sweethearts' best efforts, after a number of misunderstandings Romeo and Juliet both end up dead. In 2001, this old legend was repeated with a modern twist.

Crown Prince Dipendra of Nepal was used to getting his own way. However, the 29-year-old's parents refused to let him marry the woman he'd chosen because they didn't approve of her family. So Dipendra waited until Friday, June 1, 2001, when

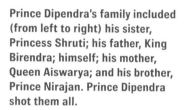

Prince Dipendra's family included (from left to right) his sister, Princess Shruti; his father, King Birendra; himself; his mother, Queen Aiswarya; and his brother, Prince Nirajan. Prince Dipendra shot them all.

he knew his family would be gathered, as they were most Friday nights, to enjoy dinner together. Prince Dipendra also knew a lot about guns, since he owned several of them and often used them in target practice.

Family members reported later that the prince had seemed a little drunk as the family collected before supper. Dipendra disappeared for a few moments, then returned. To everyone's shock and horror, he was now armed with one or two automatic rifles—no one had time to really look. The prince locked the door, then opened fire.

Nine people were murdered immediately, including Dipendra's father, mother, brother, and sister. Four others were wounded before the prince turned the gun on himself. Where were the guards and servants? Throughout the slaughter, they carefully observed court etiquette; they didn't dare get involved in what they considered "family matters."

It's hard to believe, but with the death of his father, Prince Dipendra actually became king of Nepal for the three days he lingered in a coma. When he then died, he left behind a shattered family and a tearful "Juliet."

TIMELINE

ROYAL	WHEN HE/SHE LIVED
Cleopatra	about 69–30 BCE
Mark Antony	about 83–30 BCE
Julius Caesar	about 101–44 BCE
Vlad Țepeș	1431–1476
Richard III	1452–1485
Mary I	1516–1558
Elizabeth I	1533–1603
Mary, Queen of Scots	1542–1587
Louis XVI	1754–1793
Marie Antoinette	1755–1793
Empress Elisabeth	1837–1898
Nikolay Romanov	1868–1918
Alexandra Romanova	1872–1918
Olga Romanova	1895–1918
Tatiana Romanova	1897–1918
Maria Romanova	1899–1918
Anastasia Romanova	1901–1918
Alexei Romanov	1904–1918
King Alexander I of Yugoslavia	1888–1934
Boris III, Czar of Bulgaria	1894–1943
King Abdullah Ibn Hussein of Jordan	1882–1951
King Faisal of Saudi Arabia	about 1904–1975
Louis Mountbatten	1900–1979
Crown Prince Dipendra of Nepal	1971–2001

FURTHER READING

CLEOPATRA
Gary Jeffrey and Anita Ganeri. *Cleopatra: The Life of an Egyptian Queen.* New York: The Rosen Publishing Group, 2005.
Don Nardo. *Cleopatra: Egypt's Last Pharaoh.* Farmington Hills, MI: Lucent Books (Thomson Gale, The Thomson Corp.), 2005.
Struan Reid. *Cleopatra.* Chicago: Heinemann Library (Reed Educational and Professional Publishing), 2002.
Diane Stanley. *Cleopatra.* New York: Morrow Junior Books, 1994.

VLAD ȚEPEȘ
Jim Pipe. *Dracula.* Brookfield, CT: Copper Beech Books, 1995.
Ian Thorne. *Dracula.* Mankato, MN: Crestwood House, 1977.

RICHARD III
The End of Chivalry: Henry V, Joan of Arc, Richard III. New York: M. Cavendish, 1989.

MARY I; ELIZABETH I; AND MARY, QUEEN OF SCOTS
Miriam Greenblatt. *Elizabeth I and Tudor England.* New York: Benchmark Books, 2002.
Christopher Haigh. *Elizabeth I.* Harlow, Essex, England: Pearson Education, 1998.
Hugh Brewster and Laurie Coulter. *To Be a Princess: The Fascinating Lives of Real Princesses.* Markham, ON: Scholastic Canada, 2001.
Kathryn Lasky. *Elizabeth I: Red Rose of the House of Tudor.* New York: Scholastic, 1999.

LOUIS XVI AND MARIE ANTOINETTE
Kathryn Lasky. *Marie Antoinette: Princess of Versailles.* New York: Scholastic, 2000.
Nancy Lotz and Carlene Phillips. *Marie Antoinette and the Decline of French Monarchy.* Greensboro, NC: Morgan Reynolds, 2005.
Nancy Plain. *Louis XVI, Marie Antoinette, and the French Revolution.* New York: Benchmark Books, 2002.

THE ROMANOVS
Hugh Brewster. *Anastasia's Album.* Toronto: Penguin Studio/Madison Press Books, 1996.
Kathleen Berton Murrell. *Russia.* Toronto: Stoddart, 1998.
Abraham Resnick. *Russia, a History to 1917.* Chicago: Children's Press, 1983.

MODERN MURDERS
George Fetherling. *A Biographical Dictionary of the World's Assassins.* Toronto: Random House Canada, 2001.

MAIN SOURCES

MURDER MOST ROYAL

Dulcie M. Ashdown. *Royal Murders: Hatred, Revenge and the Seizing of Power.* Stroud, Gloucestershire: Sutton Publishing, 1998.

Hugh Ross Williamson. *Historical Enigmas.* New York: St. Martin's Press, 1974.

CLEOPATRA

Ernle Bradford. *Cleopatra.* London: Penguin Books, 1971.

Edith Flamarion. *Cleopatra: The Life and Death of a Pharaoh.* New York: Harry N. Abrams, 1997.

Kristiana Gregory. *Cleopatra VII: Daughter of the Nile.* New York: Scholastic, 1999.

Don Nardo, editor. *Cleopatra.* San Diego: Greenhaven Press, 2001.

VLAD ȚEPEȘ

Radu R. Florescu. *Dracula, Prince of Many Faces: His Life and His Times.* Boston: Little, Brown, 1989.

M.J. Trow. *Vlad the Impaler: In Search of the Real Dracula.* Stroud, Gloucestershire: Sutton Publishing, 2003.

RICHARD III

Bertram Fields. *Royal Blood.* New York: HarperCollins, 1998.

Jeremy Potter. *Good King Richard.* London: Constable and Company Ltd., 1983.

Alison Weir. *The Princes in the Tower.* London: Pimlico, 1993.

Audrey Williamson. *The Mystery of the Princes.* Totowa, NJ: Rowman and Littlefield, 1978.

MARY I; ELIZABETH I; AND MARY, QUEEN OF SCOTS

Jane Dunn. *Elizabeth & Mary.* Toronto: HarperCollins, 2003.

Lacey Baldwin Smith. *Elizabeth Tudor: Portrait of a Queen.* London: Hutchinson & Co., 1976.

Alison Weir. *The Life of Elizabeth I.* New York: Ballantine Publishing Group, 1998.

LOUIS XVI AND MARIE ANTOINETTE

Annunziata Asquith. *Marie Antoinette.* London: Weidenfeld & Nicolson, 1974.

Antonia Fraser. *Marie Antoinette: The Journey.* Toronto: Doubleday, 2001.

Joan Haslip. *Marie Antoinette.* London: Weidenfeld & Nicolson, 1989.

Munro Price. *The Road from Versailles: Louis XVI, Marie Antoinette, and the Fall of the French Monarchy.* New York: St. Martin's Press, 2003.

EMPRESS ELISABETH

Brigitte Hamann. *The Reluctant Empress.* New York: Alfred A. Knopf, 1986.

Joan Haslip. *The Lonely Empress.* London: Weidenfeld & Nicolson, 1965.

Andrew Sinclair. *Death by Fame: A Life of Elisabeth, Empress of Austria.* London: Constable, 1998.

THE ROMANOVS

Alexander Grabbe. *The Private World of the Last Tsar.* Boston: Little, Brown, 1984.

Peter Kurth. *Tsar: The Lost World of Nicholas and Alexandra.* Boston: Little, Brown, 1995.

Robert K. Massie. *Nicholas and Alexandra.* New York: Atheneum, 1985.

Robert K. Massie. *The Romanovs: The Final Chapter.* New York: Random House, 1995.

MODERN MURDERS

Adaia and Abraham Shumsky. *A Bridge Across the Jordan: The Friendship Between a Jewish Carpenter and the King of Jordan.* New York: Arcade, 1997.

Philip Ziegler. *Mountbatten.* New York: Alfred A. Knopf, 1985.

Amy Willesee and Mark Whittaker. *Love and Death in Kathmandu.* New York: St. Martin's Press, 2004.

PICTURE SOURCES

Cover top right, 1, 13, 16, 18, 20, 28, 30, **34 top left**, 36, **46 top**, 48, 52, 54, 58, 60, 62, 64, 74, 76, **78 left**, 82, 86, 94, 96, **98 top**, 100, 104, **hand in glove** ©iStockphoto Inc./Tatiana Popova **knife** ©iStockphoto Inc./Robert Kohlhuber; **cover middle**, ©iStockphoto Inc./Jill Fromer; **cover bottom right**, ©iStockphoto Inc./Mollypix; 6, ©iStockphoto Inc./Juan Estey; 9, ©iStockphoto Inc./Volker Kreinacke; 14, ©iStockphoto Inc./Danilo Ascione; **34 bottom**, ©iStockphoto Inc./Kelvin Wakefield; **37 main**, ©iStockphoto Inc./Peggy De Meue; **37 background**, ©iStockphoto Inc./Ranplett; 38, ©iStockphoto Inc./John Steele; **46 bottom**, ©iStockphoto Inc./Lance Bellers; 50, ©iStockphoto Inc./Jason Walton; 57, ©iStockphoto Inc./George Cairns; 67, ©iStockphoto Inc./VanDenEsker; 71, ©iStockphoto Inc./Hulton Archive/Getty Images; 83, ©iStockphoto Inc./Christian Misje; **89 top**, ©iStockphoto Inc./Dave Logan; **89 bottom**, ©iStockphoto Inc./Stefan Hosemann; 97, ©iStockphoto Inc./Kuzma; **98 bottom**, ©iStockphoto Inc./Dainis Derics; 105, ©iStockphoto Inc./sx70; 111, ©iStockphoto Inc./Alexander Hafemann

4, 27, Courtesy Vlad Chiran

11, The Art Archive/Egyptian Museum Turin/Gianni Dagli Orti; 23, *Antoine rapporté mourant à Cléopâtre* by Ernest Hillemacher. Credit The Art Archive/Musée des Beaux Arts Grenoble/Gianni Dagli Orti; 26, *The Death of Cleopatra* by Juan Luna y Novicio. Credit The Art Archive/Fine Art Museum Bilbao/Alfredo Dagli Orti; 49, The Art Archive/Private Collection; 53, painting by Antonis Mor. Credit The Art Archive/Museo del Prado Madrid; 56, *Burning of Martin Bucer*. From *Foxe's Book of Martyr* by John Foxe, 1583 edition. Credit The Art Archive; 66, The Art Archive; 69, Painting by Lié-Louis Perin-Salbreux. Credit The Art Archive/Musée Saint Denis Reims/Gianni Dagli Orti; 75, Painting by Mme Louise-Elizabeth Vigee le Brun. Credit The Art Archive Musée du Château de Versailles/Alfredo Dagli Orti; 81, Engraving, 1793. Credit The Art Archive/Bibliothèque des Arts Décoratifs Paris/Gianni Dagli Orti; 88, Commemorative engraving. Credit The Art Archive/Museum der Stadt Wien/Alfredo Dagli Orti; 95, Engraving from *Le Petit Journal*. Credit The Art Archive/Bibliothèque Municipale Dijon/Gianni Dagli Orti; 101, 1916. Credit The Art Archive/Musée des 2 Guerres Mondiales Paris/Gianni Dagli Orti; 118, c.1945. Credit The Art Archive/Culver Pictures

17, *Triunph(us) Caesaris (The triumph of Julius Caesar)*. Chiaroscuro woodcut with gouache by Andrea Andreani after the painting by Andrea Mantegna, plate 4, 1599; 59, LC-DIG-ppmsc-07692; 65, LC-DIG-02485; 72, Photoglob Co., Zurich, LC-DIG-ppmsc-05397; **78 right**, Photoglob Co., Zurich, LC-DIG-ppmsc-05393; 80, John Davis Batchelder Collection, LC-USZ62-124552; 90, LC-DIG-ggbain-16439; 115, LC-DIG-ggbain-36558; 116, LC-DIG-matpc-12206. All courtesy Library of Congress Prints and Photographs Division

25, ©STOCKXPERT/Derocz

29, Courtesy Doctorpete, 2004

31, Erich Lessing/Art Resource, NY

32, Unattributed woodcut Strasbourg, 1500, coloured by B. Black; 42, In *Chronicle of England* by James Doyle; 47, Kronheim print in *Pictures of English History from the Earliest Times*, circa 1892, plate XLI; 92, Cartoon by Linley Sambourne for Punch's Fancy Portraits, No 22, in *Punch*, 1881. All credit Mary Evans Picture Library

34 top right, Prana-Film/The Kobal Collection

40, ©Private Collection/The Bridgeman Art Library; 55, *Queen Elizabeth I in procession with her Courtiers*, c.1600/03, from *Memoirs of the Court of Queen Elizabeth* after an oil attributed to Robert Peake. ©Private Collection/The Stapleton Collection/The Bridgeman Art Library; 108, Colour litho by S. Sarmat, 1918, from 'Histoire des Soviets' by H. de Weindel, 1923-24. ©Private Collection/Archives Charmet/The Bridgeman Art Library

43, *King Richard the Third, Act IV, scene III. Murder of the princes* by Heath after Northcote, 1791. In *The dramatic works of Shakespeare* rev. by George Steevens, 1802; 102. Both courtesy Beinecke Rare Book and Manuscript Library, Yale University

85, 1859. Courtesy Gryffindor: http://commons.wikimedia.org/wiki/Image:Empress_Elisabeth_of_Austria_Sept._2006_001.jpg

99, Photographs by A. Bajetti from the *Illustrierte Zeitung*, 1901. Courtesy Mrlopez2681

113, AP/World Wide Photo; 117, AP/World Wide Photo

120, ©Kapoor Baldev/Sygma/CORBIS

ACKNOWLEDGMENTS

Thanks to the many people who helped me with this book, including librarians at the Toronto Reference Library and the Northern District Branch.

I really appreciate the support of everyone at Annick Press, especially Rick Wilks and Brigitte Waisberg. Very special thanks to the amazing designer Sheryl Shapiro and Sandra Booth, an incredible photo researcher. I am also extremely grateful to editors Barbara Pulling and Heather Sangster.

Thank you, Lynn and Graham, for your interest in this book. Many thanks to Dad, John and Douglas. With love always to Paul for his help and support— and no, this isn't a how-to book!

INDEX

We acknowledge the support of the Canada Council for the Arts,
the Ontario Arts Council, and the Government of Canada through
the Book Publishing Industry Development Program (BPIDP) for
our publishing activities.

 ONTARIO ARTS COUNCIL
CONSEIL DES ARTS DE L'ONTARIO

Cataloging in Publication

MacLeod, Elizabeth
    Royal murder : the deadly intrigue of ten sovereigns / by Elizabeth MacLeod.

Includes bibliographical references and index.
ISBN 978-1-55451-127-3 (pbk.).—ISBN 978-1-55451-128-0 (bound)

    1. Kings and rulers—Assassination—Juvenile literature. 2. Assassination—
Juvenile literature. I. Title.

HV6278.M334 2008   j364.1524   C2007-907294-1

Distributed in Canada by:
Firefly Books Ltd.
66 Leek Crescent
Richmond Hill, ON
L4B 1H1

Published in the U.S.A. by:
Annick Press (U.S.) Ltd.
Distributed in the U.S.A. by:
Firefly Books (U.S.) Inc.
P.O. Box 1338
Ellicott Station
Buffalo, NY 14205

Printed in China.

Visit us at: www.annickpress.com

The evening sky darkens,
The campfire aglow,
Ghost stories in the tepee,
From these two just flow.

Dedicated to Abi & Mia,
fearless storytellers on the IOW
—Graham and Lynn